V I R G I N I A   W O O L F

Virginia Woolf

BY DAVID DAICHES

A NEW DIRECTIONS PAPERBOOK

MANUFACTURED IN THE UNITED STATES OF AMERICA
BY THE VAIL-BALLOU PRESS INC., BINGHAMTON, N.Y.

NEW DIRECTIONS BOOKS ARE PUBLISHED BY JAMES LAUGHLIN AT
NORFOLK, CONNECTICUT. NEW YORK OFFICE: 333 SIXTH AVENUE (14)

To my Wife

*For her patience
in letting me ventilate my theories
about literature in conversations with her;
and for profounder reasons.*

ACKNOWLEDGMENT

The selections from Virginia Woolf's works quoted herein are used by kind permission of Harcourt, Brace & Co., Inc., who publish the following books by Mrs. Woolf:

Fiction

MONDAY OR TUESDAY

THE VOYAGE OUT

NIGHT AND DAY

JACOB'S ROOM

MRS. DALLOWAY

TO THE LIGHTHOUSE

ORLANDO

THE WAVES

THE YEARS

BETWEEN THE ACTS

Biography

FLUSH: A BIOGRAPHY

ROGER FRY

Criticism

THE COMMON READER

THE SECOND COMMON READER

A ROOM OF ONE'S OWN

THREE GUINEAS

THE DEATH OF THE MOTH AND OTHER ESSAYS

CONTENTS

PREFACE TO THE SECOND
EDITION

PREFACE TO SECOND EDITION

THIS BOOK WAS WRITTEN OVER TWENTY YEARS AGO IN RE-
sponse to an invitation from James Laughlin to contribute
a volume to his newly launched "Makers of Modern Literature" series. It was barely begun when the unexpected
and shocking news of Virginia Woolf's death was an-
nounced. This seemed to emphasise the necessity for describing and evaluating her achievement, for summing
up the meaning and significance of her work. My study
was thus presented as a preliminary clarification, a first
attempt to "place" Virginia Woolf as a novelist. I am all
too aware now that in many respects it is over-schematic
and at some points over-simplified. If I were to write a
book about Virginia Woolf now, my whole approach
would be different. I should begin with a careful analysis
of *Mrs. Dalloway*, which I now see as the most central
and in a sense the most *fulfilled* of all her novels, and
then proceed to use the ideas developed in that analysis
in discussing her approach to fiction and her other works.
I would of course have the advantage of those illuminat-

ing selections from her journal, published by her husband under the title *A Writer's Diary* in 1953, which provide such important clues to the way in which her imagination worked. I do not think that I would need to modify anything in the light of her other posthumously published writings which appeared after my book was written—*The Death of the Moth* (1942), *The Moment and Other Essays* (1942), *The Captain's Death-Bed* (1950), and *Granite and Rainbow* (1958)—for these sketches and critical essays, interesting though they are, reveal no new side of her talent and contain nothing that was not at least as well done in books published during her lifetime. I would not even—and I must say this though it may sound arrogant—modify my general view in response to the criticism of Virginia Woolf that has appeared since 1942, for it is my own re-reading of and meditation on her work rather than anybody else's views, however persuasively argued, that have given me what I believe to be a richer understanding of her novels and a clearer discernment of exactly what she was doing. My views of Conrad and of Joyce have been considerably changed and subtilized since I first wrote about those two novelists in my book on the modern novel published in 1939, and this has been very largely as a result of the great amount of helpful new criticism that has appeared. By contrast, my views of Virginia Woolf have developed in isolation. Perhaps that has something to do with the kind of novelist she is. At any rate, my sense of the inadequacies of this twenty-year-old study derives more from my own brooding than from the impact of the limited amount of criticism that has appeared.

If I think the book has faults, it might be asked, why have I not radically revised it? My answer is simply that a book of this kind cannot be revised, only completely re-written. And I believe that this "hand-book" approach, with all its limitations, can still be of use, and that the general position it takes up is sound, its stresses right, its signposts pointed in the right direction. The one real correction in interpretation I now wish to make—or perhaps it is only a shift in emphasis—concerns *Mrs. Dalloway*. On reading over now what I wrote about this novel, I find that I paid a great deal of attention to the technical devices employed but did not sufficiently explain what those devices were employed *for*. I am convinced now that *Mrs. Dalloway*, like so much of Mrs. Woolf's work, is essentially about the unresolvable paradox involved in the individual's need to retain his individuality while at the same time needing some real communion with others. The theme of Septimus Warren Smith, the mentally deranged young man whose derangement consists in his inability to be aware of the reality of other people and who is bullied into a semblance of communion with others—a mechanical outward conformity—by the two doctors, is basic to the story. It is only when Sir William Bradshaw, the doctor whose stultifying insistence on outward conformity to upper-class social habit has already (we are told quite clearly) destroyed his wife before it goes on to destroy Warren Smith—it is only when he appears at Mrs. Dalloway's party, tells his story, and arouses Mrs. Dalloway's deep revulsion and a sense in her of an identity with Warren Smith, that the strands of the novel at last begin to come together. For Mrs. Dalloway too is

xiii

obsessed by the need for true communion and is dissat-isfied with its simulacrum. She had rejected an offer of marriage from Peter Walsh because his dominant person-ality would have left no room for the exercise of her own, and married Dalloway because he left her more freedom as a person: yet that freedom is a kind of isolation, and she is haunted continually by thoughts and images that suggest that she has been left alone—in a narrow grave, in a lonely tower, behind a wall.

The novel begins and ends with Mrs. Dalloway's party. Why a *party?* Because parties bring people together. But they also emphasize the fact that people brought together on a purely social occasion may not be able to achieve real communion at all. Mrs. Dalloway looks out of her window to see the old lady opposite making ready to go upstairs to bed—"climb up the narrow winding stair to bed," in Yeats's image of life's progress towards death—and feels both divided from and united with her. (Win-dows, the invisible walls which divide us from each other, are also effectively used in this way in *To the Lighthouse.*) Meanwhile, the party is going on. At the very end of the book, Peter Walsh, whose coming to the party (from India) brings Mrs. Dalloway's past, as well as his own, concretely into the present moment, is re-deemed from his intent preoccupation with his own mem-ories and reactions by a vivid, exciting awareness that Mrs. Dalloway is there, in all *her* individuality, in all her otherness:

> It is Clarissa, he said.
> For there she was.

That is how the novel ends, not only in an assertion of the moment in the midst of flux—and in my original discussion I perhaps sufficiently stressed the dialectical opposition between the flux of time and the moment in Mrs. Woolf's work—but in an assertion of individuality in the midst of society. Earlier in the novel Mrs. Dalloway had speculated on what happens to what is not ourselves when we ourselves die. Does the outside world depend for its reality on our awareness of it? That would put an intolerable burden on selfhood. Better to imagine that death solves the problem of identity and communion by making us all truly members of one another:

> Did it matter then, she asked herself, walking towards Bond Street did it matter that she must inevitably cease completely; all this must go on without her; did she resent it; or did it not become consoling to believe that death ended absolutely? but that somehow in the streets of London, on the ebb and flow of things, here, there she survived, Peter survived, lived in each other, she being part, she was positive, of the trees at home; of the house there, ugly, rambling all to bits and pieces as it was; part of people she had never met; being laid out like a mist between the people she knew best, who lifted her on their branches as she had seen the trees lift the mist, but it spread ever so far, her life, herself.

And at that moment she sees in a bookseller's window a copy of Shakespeare open at

> Fear no more the heat o' the sun
> Nor the furious winter's rages.

This introduces the theme of the lonely grave, repeated in so many different ways throughout the novel; death may not be the ultimate in communion but rather the ultimate in loneliness. Both possibilities haunt Mrs. Dalloway's mind and are related, in the emotional rhythm of the novel, to the main theme of the relation between individuality and communion and between the moment and the flux of time.

One would have to concede that the kind of sensibility cultivated by Virginia Woolf was the product of leisure and a special kind of education, but to attack her and her novels because this is so is surely irrational. Many of the most valuable productions of civilization derive from leisure and a special kind of education. The attack on Virginia Woolf as a representative of upper-class Bloomsbury sophistication, of the kind of thing that D. H. Lawrence so memorably hit out against, betrays its prejudice by its very terms. The question is, how interesting, significant, memorable, moving, is Virginia Woolf's presentation of her insights into the predicaments of human consciousness, not how exclusive or socially and intellectually narrow some of her friends may have been. Twenty years ago I protested against the habit of looking at Virginia Woolf through her Bloomsbury environment. Most of us now know considerably more about the Bloomsbury Group than we knew then—thanks largely to J. K. Johnstone's book on the subject (1954)—but this only makes the habit of seeing Mrs. Woolf as a member of this group even easier to fall into. It is her novels that matter—particularly, I would claim, *Mrs. Dalloway, To the Lighthouse,* and *Between the Acts.* (I may have been ungenerous to *The Waves* in my book, but I still feel that the excessive stylization does not fully come off. I think more of *Jacob's Room* the more I read it.) The delicate move-

xvi

ment of her prose rhythms, suggesting, evoking, illuminating, seems to me to be a remarkable achievement;
more and more in reading her beautifully modulated
transcriptions of consciousness at bay I have the feeling
that here is the definite rendering of a particular kind of
modern sensibility, of modern dilemma, and that I know
it and respond to it with a deep inward response. Some
critics have argued that her symbolism leads nowhere,
the awareness of her characters is altogether too precious
and contrived, her whole world is too preposterously
rarefied. To which in the last analysis all I can reply is
that I do not find it so. One hesitates to fall back on mere
autobiographical response as a means of critical defence,
but it is justified up to a point by what appears to be the
fact that there are two radically different kinds of response to Virginia Woolf's work, and both are found
among intelligent readers. One response is to see the
novels as a kind of intellectual game and try desperately
to make the images and symbols add up; sometimes the
attempt is successful, sometimes it is unsuccessful. The
other is to start from the deeply felt conviction, achieved
in reading, that they *do* add up, and to try and find out
not *whether* they do but *why* they do. It is the second
kind of reader who feels his disturbed consent wrung
from him as he reads, who watches fascinated as he sees
his own hitherto unarticulated and unrealised moods and
intuitions contained in a work of literary art. I make no
apology for thus emphasising the human significance, the
capacity for moving and revealing, that I find in Virginia
Woolf's novels. Far too much modern criticism is con-

cerned merely with working out the puzzle and too little with inquiry into the reasons why the puzzle (if it is a puzzle) is worth working out in the first place.

I never knew Virginia Woolf, and it was only after my book was written that I came into contact with people who had known her, and learned more about her life and environment than I then knew. Not only do I now know more about the intellectual background in which she was brought up—Noel Annan's *Leslie Stephen: his Thought and Character in Relation to his Time* (1951) was an important help here—but I realize now that I underestimated the degree to which characters she had known and the events of her own life played a part in her fiction. The quotation on page 46 refers, as I now know, to "the great dreadnaught hoax," when young Virginia Stephen and her brothers fooled some of the highest brass in the Royal Navy. There is more of Leslie Stephen in Mr. Ramsay of *To the Lighthouse* than I first realized. She introduced private jokes and private knowledge into many of her works. But an awareness of all this does not alter in any significant way the manner in which we read her books and how we judge them. My comment that "she did better in writing about characters she had never known except through her imagination" (p. 152) might perhaps be modified to read: "She did better when her imagination was free to work as it would on the material she derived from life." But my main point, that she showed her distinctive qualities less in writing the biography of a friend than in writing novels in which facts about some of her friends may have been utilized, is not affected.

xviii

PREFACE TO SECOND EDITION

The text that follows has, for reasons which I have tried to explain, not been altered, except for the bibliography, which has been brought up to date.

School of English and American Studies,
University of Sussex.   David Daiches.

1. MAINLY BIOGRAPHICAL

VIRGINIA WOOLF WAS BORN IN LONDON IN 1882. HER FATHER was Leslie Stephen, the distinguished critic, biographer, philosopher and scholar, who lived from 1832 to 1904 and was on friendly terms with almost all the great Victorian writers. He had given up an assured future at Cambridge because he felt his agnosticism to be incompatible with the professions required at that time of a Cambridge don, and settled in London in 1864 where he embarked on a career as literary journalist, critic and editor, among whose monuments are the *Dictionary of National Biography* and his *History of English Thought in the Eighteenth Century*. Altogether he published over thirty volumes, mostly biographical and critical, in addition to his vast editorial work. Sensitive, honest and thoughtful, Leslie Stephen moved with distinction if not always with confidence among the literary men of his age, and his children were brought up in an atmosphere both literary and scholarly. His first wife was Thackeray's daughter: she died, leav-

1

ing one daughter, after eight years of happy marriage. After three unhappy years he married again, equally successfully. His second wife, Mrs. Julia Prinsep Jackson Duckworth, the widow of a barrister whom Stephen had known well, bore him four children, Vanessa, Julian Thoby, Virginia and Adrian. It was of the second Mrs. Stephen that George Meredith said, "I never reverenced a woman more." She came of a family that was, according to her daughter Virginia, "extremely frivolous and art-loving and sociable" and was quite a beauty in her day. She died in 1895.

Brought up as a member of a large and talented family (for the second Mrs. Stephen had children by her first marriage, who were brought up with the Stephens) Virginia moved throughout her childhood in a world that was both self-contained and exciting. Her education was informal and unusually rich. Her father's magnificent library was her only university, and she made the fullest use of it. Self-educated in the best sense, she familiarized herself in her own time and her own way with her father's vast collection of English and classical works (which included a particularly fine eighteenth century collection). She grew up to take culture for granted. Nearly all the characters in her novels are persons of unusual culture, and it never seems to have occurred to her that the vast majority of the population of Britain had not enjoyed the classics and could not read a foreign language. She inherited her father's intellectual honesty and moral integrity, and was an intellectual snob deliberately and without hypocrisy, as a means of communicating her belief in the importance of intelligence. One thing she never

2

could have learned in her father's well-stocked library was to suffer fools gladly. She learned Greek from Walter Pater's sister, and like Katherine Hilbery in *Night and Day* was patted on the head as a child by many an eminent Victorian. The leather smell of her father's study, as well as the actual characters of the scholar and his wife, are to be found in all her early novels. To the end of her life her sensibility was based on intelligence.

After his second marriage Leslie Stephen regularly spent his summer holidays in Cornwall, a part of the country for which he developed a great affection. In 1881 he bought a house at St. Ives and the family went there every summer for thirteen years without a break. Cornwall, therefore, as well as London, was the scene of Virginia's childhood and youth. London and the sea both haunt her adult imagination, and as a rule the setting of her novels is either in the city or on a lonely coast. *Jacob's Room* opens in Cornwall and moves to London. *Mrs. Dalloway* is set wholly in London. In *To the Lighthouse* the characters are set throughout on the north western Scottish coast whose flavour and atmosphere are as much Cornwallesque as Hebridean. Indeed, this antithesis between the city and the shore, between London and Cornwall, is almost symbolic of the nature of her sensibility, which contemplates the solid facts of life with the meditative eye that has learned its introspective and dissolving wisdom from watching sunsets over deserted seas. One might even push the symbolic contrast further, and see an opposition between reason, London, and her paternal heredity on the one hand, and intuition, Cornwall and the legacy of her mother's family on the other. The combination of these two sets of opposites produced her unique kind of vision.

Leslie Stephen sloughed off his traditional religious orthodoxy at a comparatively early age, and without any violent mental struggle. Throughout his later life he preserved an attitude of reasonable agnosticism which he employed to reinforce rather than break down a very strong moral sense and a genuine feeling for domesticity. This had its effect on his children. Virginia was brought up not as a militant atheist nor even as a sceptic, but as a rational moralist whose duty was to seek and hold fast to the truth as she saw it. That sense of personal vision which we note in all her fiction has its points of similarity with her father's independence of mind.

After her father's death in 1904 Virginia, with her sister Vanessa and her two brothers, settled at 46 Gordon Square, Bloomsbury, where, independent, talented, and with an income of her own (the Stephens had been very comfortably off) she first turned her hand to writing. In 1907, after Vanessa married Clive Bell, the art critic, Virginia and her brother Adrian took a house together at 29 Fitzroy Square. Virginia had her own workroom upstairs, but it was in Adrian's book-lined study on the ground floor that their friends gathered at night for whisky, buns, cocoa and conversation. Virginia herself did more listening than talking. Among the regular visitors at Fitzroy Square were Desmond Macarthy, Charles Tennyson, Clive Bell, Lytton Strachey, Hilton Young and John Maynard Keynes. It was here that the so-called "Bloomsbury Group" had its origins. "I do not think," says one who knew her then, "that her new existence had 'become alive' to Virginia's imagination in those first years. She gave the impression of being so intensely receptive to any experience new to her, and so intensely interested in facts that she had not come across before, that time was necessary to give it meaning as a whole. It took the years to complete her vision of it." [1]

The lack of constraint, the sense of freedom, made possible by her circumstances encouraged her to write as she pleased. But it was a long time before she felt herself sufficiently prepared to engage in creative writing. Her early work is all critical, and it was through her criticism that she developed her ideas about writing. She became a reviewer for the *Times Literary Supplement* (and continued one until her death) besides publishing a great deal of free-lance criticism in other periodicals both British and American. She kept on reading widely; she travelled abroad; and, in 1912, she married.

She was fortunate in her marriage. Her husband, Leonard Woolf, journalist, publicist, political thinker and general essayist, was a man of lively and sympathetic mind, keenly interested in literature and indeed in almost everything, and sufficiently aware of his wife's talent to encourage her from the first in her career as a writer. He was two years her senior, a distinguished graduate of Trinity College, Cambridge, who had served seven years (1904–1911) in the Ceylon Civil Service and had returned to England with some very definite ideas about British colonial policy and related questions. In the course of a distinguished career he was to display his versatile talents in many fields, his writings ranging from a bitter

[1] Duncan Grant in *Horizon*, June, 1941.

analysis of Britain's policy towards the black races in Africa to fiction, of which at least one example, *The Village in the Jungle,* is quite outstanding. The marriage of a woman of genius to a man of great talent ought by all the laws to have ended in a mess. But Leonard Woolf was no Thomas Carlyle, nor was Virginia a Jane Welsh. In 1915, after seven years of work, she published her first novel.

Throughout her life she moved in an environment which, if as a rule outwardly placid, was full of intellectual excitement. The gatherings at Gordon Square and Fitzroy Square represented a type of intellectual sociability which she kept encouraging. She was always interested in people, remarking many times during the last ten years of her life that she preferred reading autobiography to fiction. "It was therefore not surprising to see her, at one time and another, in that upper room in Tavistock Square, happy in the company of, for example, Lytton Strachey, Lowes Dickinson, Roger Fry, E. M. Forster, T. S. Eliot, Stephen Spender, Elizabeth Bowen, or Rosamund Lehmann. She had a great gift for making the young and obscure feel that they were of great value too; she admired physical as well as intellectual beauty; she could charm away diffidence; and she could be notably sympathetic with young women, particularly young women from Cambridge. A strong sense of the proper functions of literature and the importance of taste gave her a proper pride (derived doubtless in part from her literary father and background) in her own gifts, but she was absolutely without arrogance." [1]

[1] William Plomer in *Horizon,* May, 1941.

In 1917 the Woolfs founded the Hogarth Press, which developed from a small hand press into the successful publishing house that has brought out some of the most interesting literature of our time, including Virginia Woolf's own novels. She herself acted as publisher's reader and read a great number of manuscripts. Writing, reading, publishing, conversing, she led a life that was intellectually active in the highest degree, and, as time was to show, proved more exhausting than observers realized. Those who did not know her and were perhaps a little jealous of her position in the literary world referred to her as the leader of the "Bloomsbury Group," but this is an unfair and misleading description. The term was bandied about by journalists and minor critics as denoting a peculiarly highbrow and self-conscious type of literary preciosity. Actually, Virginia Woolf was part of no such literary movement, and the term "Bloomsbury" in this connection is a distortion founded on a topographical accident. The matter has been well summed up by T. S. Eliot: "Any group will appear more uniform, and probably more intolerant and exclusive from the outside than it really is; and here, certainly, no subscription of orthodoxy was imposed. Had it, indeed, been a matter of limited membership and exclusive doctrine, it would not have attracted the exasperated attention of those who objected to it on these supposed grounds . . . I only mention the matter in order to make the point that Virginia Woolf was the centre, not merely of an esoteric group, but of the literary life of London. Her position was due to a concurrence of qualities and circumstances which never happened before, and which I do not think will ever happen again. It maintained the dignified and admirable tradition of Victorian upper middle-class culture—a situation in which the artist was neither the servant of the exalted patron, the parasite of the plutocrat, nor the entertainer of the mob—a situation in which the producer and the consumer of art were on an equal footing, and that neither the highest nor the lowest." [1]

Such were the circumstances of Virginia Woolf's early and middle life. Before completing this story, let us turn from her life to her work.

[1] *Horizon,* May, 1941.

2. EARLY NOVELS

THE VOYAGE OUT, VIRGINIA WOOLF'S FIRST NOVEL, WAS PUB-
lished in 1915. While conforming in structure and external pretensions to the traditions of fiction writing which
the nineteenth century had bequeathed to the twentieth,
it already showed signs of the author's search for a more
delicate savouring of experience than the traditional
novel allowed. There is a plot, of sorts. Characters are
brought into relations with each other and in the process
things happen, complications arise and are resolved, and
in the course of all this personalities are described and
analyzed. But if we inquire into the exact nature of the
plot, the quality of the experiences described, the meaning of the final resolution, we find that the entire meaning of the novel seems to be on a different level than that
of the generality of works of fiction that had preceded this.
The story centres on Rachel Vinrace, an immature and
inexperienced girl, who, in the course of a voyage on her
father's boat, the *Euphrosyne*, and a subsequent stay with
her aunt and uncle in their house on the "lonely little is-

land" of Santa Marina, learns something about the world and in particular about the relation between the sexes: she finally completes her education by falling in love, and soon after dies of a tropical fever. There is little action and hardly any suspense in the book, which moves slowly onward, picking out moments of introspection or conversations that reveal, in greater or less degree, the subtleties of personality. Of the older novelists, Meredith might have done something like this, but he would have had a great deal more action, and his insights would have been less tenuous—he would have knocked a more concrete truth out of his characters before he had finished with them. Henry James, too, might have lingered in the same way over apparently aimless conversations or slowed down the narrative to probe delicately into dim emotions, but the atmosphere of his novel would have been clearer and brighter, and the structure more finely organized.

There is a hesitancy, even a clumsiness, in *The Voyage Out,* which denotes the writer who has not yet found her proper medium. Again and again we find Virginia Woolf hovering over her subject, undecided where to pounce, until the chapter is filled up with a miscellaneous collection of descriptions and digressions which do not seem to lead anywhere. The minor characters in the book keep changing their size constantly: sometimes they are full-sized personalities, on whom the author is concentrating all her powers of description and analysis, and soon after they become mere background figures, whose only function seems to be to bring out certain reactions in others. Mr. and Mrs. Ambrose (the professor and his wife, prototype of the Ramsays in *To the Lighthouse,* characters who

10

seem to carry with them the atmosphere of Leslie Ste-phen's study) oscillate from background to foreground; Mrs. Ambrose in particular, the efficient wife of the pre-occupied academic and Rachel's aunt, is elaborated up to a point where we expect her to dominate the book, and is finally left vaguely in the background, while her husband is abandoned altogether. Mr. and Mrs. Richard Dalloway (the same who reappear, older and more complete, in *Mrs. Dalloway*) are brought in and eyed meditatively, only to be completely dismissed in the first quarter of the book, having served their function, apparently, in arousing certain reactions in Rachel. The author never seems quite sure what she wants of her characters, and they tend to become mere excuses for tenuous meditation or some-what lumpish exercises in observation and psychological analysis. What, the critic inquires, is the view of fiction implicit in a work of this kind?

It is a view that is not easy to define. Virginia Woolf has here assembled a number of characters and allowed herself to contemplate their behaviour and their emotions throughout a succession of events which are not, on any usual standard, exciting, and which end, by way of a con-clusion of the pattern, in the death of the character on whom the author has focussed most of her attention. There is a unity in the book, in so far as the centre of in-terest remains Rachel Vinrace; but observations of other characters are not subordinated to that main theme, and the novel contains a large number of independent insights, as though the author had, for diversion, taken her eyes off her principal subject occasionally, and turned them in calm inquiry on whoever happened to be available. It is

11

clear that "plot" in the traditional sense has no interest for this writer. The story is carried forward to a conclusion, the events are marshalled in a coherent order, development does take place, but the reader feels that all this is a concession to convention, and that the real interest derives from the quality of observation the novelist brings to bear now on this subject, now on that. The pattern is concluded because the author appears to be tired of looking in that particular direction, and lifts her gaze. Rachel Vinrace is sent to her death because for the moment Virginia Woolf can see no more of the quality of life by meditating on her further—and also, it might be added, because death for this writer was always the illuminator of and commentator on life, so that an adequate insight into any character is only given if he is shown not only living but also in some connection with death. This is true, as we shall see, of Jacob Flanders in *Jacob's Room,* of Mrs. Dalloway, of Mrs. Ramsay in *To the Lighthouse,* and of the principal characters of all her other novels.

Can we say, then, that Virginia Woolf's main interest in this book is metaphysical rather than literary? It is true that she seems more intent on recording some subtle insights into the nature of experience than in writing the traditional kind of novel, but on the other hand the metaphysical and the literary constitute no real pair of contraries. Philosophical insight may be, and has often been, successfully conveyed through fiction, and whatever else literary value may be it may certainly in some of its aspects include the philosophical. Some types of literature are obviously imaginative patterns of experience constructed in order to record and illustrate insights that

12

might well be called metaphysical. The differentiating quality of literature lies not in its end—for it may share its end with philosophy or science, or its end may be merely sensational—but in the means employed to achieve that end. A philosophical novel has as much chance of being a good piece of literature as has a naturalistic one, and George Eliot and Henry James are no less writers of fiction than Balzac and Zola.

To say that Virginia Woolf is concerned with conveying to the reader, through a "story," fitful gleams of insight into the subtler realms of human consciousness, is not necessarily to remove her outside the tradition of English or European fiction. Samuel Richardson, no philosopher and certainly not a man of over subtle instincts, had done something which might be defined in just that way. What is it, then, that strikes the reader of *The Voyage Out* as outside the tradition of previous English fiction, that makes him suspect that the particular form employed— the record of a series of events that happened to a number of people during a selected period of time—is not really the proper form for the content, and that the work was hardly intended to be what it turned out to be?

The fact is, that in the traditional novel what the author has to say can only be said through the arrangement and patterning of a chronological series of events: in *Tom Jones*, as in *The Egoist*, the novel is *what happens*. But what Virginia Woolf wants to say seems to be only casually linked to any chronological series of events: we feel in this novel that she could have illuminated her subject just as well by standing still as by moving forward. The traditional handling of time-sequence, in fact, seems to this novelist to be incidental, while the older novelists found it essential. Rachel Vinrace develops from immaturity to experience, and thence quietly to death, but the kind of meaning that Virginia Woolf is trying to get across to the reader does not really derive from that development, though at first sight it appears to. If we try to analyze the novel on traditional lines, tracing out the development, complication and resolution of the plot, we may find ourselves with a neat piece of analysis, but we shall certainly have missed the essential novel that Virginia Woolf was writing.

It is not that Virginia Woolf is concerned with timeless entities, but rather that her insights into experience depend on making patterns within time that do not depend on chronology. It strikes the careful reader of *The Voyage Out* that had the author been free to use the fact of the heroine's eventual death throughout the book, instead of waiting until it took place, she would have presented her vision more clearly. For throughout the book something is continually breaking up the solidarity of events; the characters suddenly cease being real and become more and more fantastic, then lurch back into reality again; memory crowds the present and temporarily annihilates it; people become looming symbols in a fog of dissolving facts. But there is the story to take up, the events to follow in due order, and the result is that the world of shifting and dissolving things is continually being pushed away to make room for the solid march of events. And so the reader wonders which he ought to believe—chronology, or the luminous fog that keeps interrupting it. In other words, there seems to be a struggle between the form of

14

the book and the content. Social events and situations that seem to come straight out of Jane Austen merge into moods and dimnesses that would have baffled Jane completely.

One must, of course, beware of reading into this early novel qualities that we find only when we have read the later ones. *The Voyage Out* is on the surface a conventional and even uninteresting story of a group of intellectuals and society folk and others, centring on the events that happen to an immature girl who develops sufficiently to fall in love before dying of fever. There is no new contribution to English fiction here. But the reader does note a quality that can best be described as sensitivity, an ability on the part of the author to explore the implications of the individual action or gesture, so that nothing is allowed to slip by before it has been assimilated into the insubstantial texture of the book. What faintly disturbs the reader is that there seems to be no identifiable point of view directing this process of assimilation: actions dissolve into the flux of experience under the author's gaze, but the dissolving agent—to extend the metaphor—seems to be now this acid, now that. Life responds to delicate brooding, Virginia Woolf seems to be insisting, *any* kind of brooding, so long as it is sensitive and persistent. Thus in spite of what, in traditional terms, appears to be a clearly defined theme—the development of the heroine from immaturity to maturity and death—on closer reading the book appears to lack direction and unity: indeed, a specious unity seems to be given to it by this process of breaking down one action after another into something that is not what it seems. Facts may be attacked by irony, by meditation, by introspection, or by delicately shifting dialogue, and no principle seems to determine which weapon is to be used on which occasion. Anything to break down the material, anything to produce a significance other than the surface one, would appear to be Virginia Woolf's aim, and we get a story with action and plot in the conventional sense, a story which by its *form* depends for its meaning on the sequence of events, whose real meaning nevertheless depends on the author's throwing, by a variety of devices, all sorts of contradictory meanings into the *content*. Thus the story opens with Mrs. Ambrose grieving over her leaving her children, and ends far away from Mrs. Ambrose, with the reactions of a group of minor characters to Rachel's death. The opening passage, which is a careful and subtle piece of writing, does not put its care and subtlety at the service of any single interpretation or patterning of the total series of events. It is clear that the author is concerned in some way with the discrepancy between appearance and reality, and in this book if she can present this discrepancy (or a sense of it) with reference to a group of chronological events she does not mind if the chronology turns out in the long run to be irrelevant. The reader is tempted, at this stage, to ask whether fiction is really this writer's *métier*.

And the answer to this question depends on how we define the term 'fiction.' Just what fiction is—what is its nature and scope, its sphere and function—is a query we must beware of answering in too *a priori* a fashion if we wish to understand and appreciate some of the most interesting writing of the present century. For a variety of reasons, the scope of fiction has been extended in this century, the novel has attempted to do kinds of things it had never done before. Virginia Woolf is one of those who, paradoxically, by limiting the subject and scope of her novels, managed to extend the definition of fiction beyond that which had been accepted by her predecessors from Defoe to Galsworthy. She stands with James Joyce and a very few others among those who, by working out new techniques for the accomplishment of objectives at once more limited and (some at least would maintain) more subtle than those aimed at by previous writers of fiction, permanently enlarged the definition of the novel. But this is to anticipate: let us return to her early work.

Virginia Woolf's second novel, *Night and Day,* appeared in 1919. It is an elaborate study of an intelligent upper middle-class young woman passing from the rejection of one lover to the acceptance of another. Katharine Hilbery, the heroine, granddaughter of a famous poet whose memory still dominates the life of the whole Hilbery family, is portrayed as a sensitive and high spirited intellectual who conforms to no normal feminine pattern, who is, in fact, more than a trifle masculine by nature and temperament, with a secret love of mathematics and astronomy and habits of solitary speculation that produce in her friends an attitude of slightly puzzled respect. The book opens amid the rattle of teacups, in an atmosphere that the unwary reader may interpret as an introduction to a Jane Austen type of social comedy:

It was a Sunday evening in October, and in common with many other young ladies of her class, Katharine Hilbery was pouring out tea. Perhaps a fifth of her mind was thus occupied, and the remaining parts leapt over the little barrier of day which inter-

17

posed between Monday morning and this rather subdued moment, and played with the things one does voluntarily and normally in the daylight. But although she was silent, she was evidently mistress of a situation which was familiar enough to her, and inclined to let it take its way for the six hundredth time, perhaps, without bringing into play any of her unoccupied faculties. A single glance was enough to show that Mrs. Hilbery was so rich in the gifts which make tea-parties of elderly distinguished people successful, that she scarcely needed any help from her daughter, provided that the tiresome business of teacups and bread and butter was discharged for her.

Considering that the little party had been seated round the tea-table for less than twenty minutes, the animation observable on their faces, and the amount of sound they were producing collectively, were very creditable to the hostess.

It looks, from this beginning, as though Katharine Hilbery is to be built up into an Emma Woodhouse or an Elizabeth Bennett—a young lady both good-looking and intelligent who, after coming into conflict with the less intelligent aspects of her social milieu, ends by marrying a rather saturnine highbrow and finding all her problems solved. And on one level the story as it unfolds is not so unlike this pattern. But the social comedy that seems to determine the superficial form of the book is not its essence, and the Jane Austen attitude of mildly satiric observation is overwhelmed so regularly in a groping towards a profounder interpretation of the subtler and more evanescent aspects of human psychology that the reader is soon led to abandon the frame of mind which the opening paragraphs induced in him in favour of one which accepts as premise the superior importance of introspection to either description or narrative.

Katharine Hilbery is a stronger figure than any of Jane

Austen's heroines, with a firmer grip on her own destiny and a much greater curiosity about life and her own relation to it. Living in a household devoted largely to the celebration of her famous grandfather's memory, with a mother—the great poet's daughter—who, though vague, has a picturesquely sensitive disposition and an unquenchable love of the English classics combined with a certain indirect efficiency in managing practical affairs, and a father who is both a scholar and a gentleman, Katharine moves in an atmosphere of intellectual refinement which makes every afternoon tea a literary *conversazione* and every casual remark about the day's routine duties a piece of literary criticism. She and her mother are engaged in writing a full-length biography of her grandfather, but her mother's lack of method and her own preference of mathematics to poetry conspire to prevent the work from making much progress. The whole atmosphere is charged with a spirit of well-bred intelligence, and more and more Katharine Hilbery reminds us of Virginia Stephen, moving in an urbane environment of scholarship and philosophy with her distinguished father and his friends.

On Katharine's existence as the heir to a distinguished literary and social tradition there impinge four other persons: William Rodney, elegant, precise, scholarly, vain, frequenter of the Hilbery tea-parties and member of the same social class; Ralph Denham, poor but brilliant lawyer who lives with a widowed mother and an indecently large number of brothers and sisters in a somewhat delapidated house in Highgate (the Hilberys live in Cheyne Walk); Mary Datchet, unwealthy but independent feminist, who works for women's suffrage and lives alone in a top flat in an unidentified part of London; and Cassandra Otway, young, volatile, unsophisticated country cousin of Katharine's.

The story opens with William Rodney on the point of becoming engaged to Katharine, while Ralph Denham is interested in both Katharine and Mary. William and Katharine eventually become engaged, but his fussiness and vanity irk her and her critical attitude hurts him, and the reader knows from the beginning that the engagement will not last. Ralph reacts to the engagement of these two by offering himself to Mary Datchet who, though she has fallen in love with him, is too wise to accept a man who offers marriage under such circumstances. The situation is saved by Cassandra who, on a visit to the Hilberys in London, arouses William Rodney's love by her unaffected enthusiasm for his abilities. After several complications William and Katharine conspire to effect William's engagement to Cassandra, which leaves Katharine free to marry Ralph: and this, after a great deal of talk and thought, she eventually does, leaving Mary Datchet, alone but no longer unhappy, working triumphantly for the cause of democracy in her top story room above the London streets. The devices employed for bringing the characters together are fairly crude, and the actual moments of crisis and decision are indistinctly recorded: the main interest of the story lies in the conversations, speculations and introspections in which the characters, and principally Katharine Hilbery, continually engage during those moments of doubt and hesitation which are so fully recorded.

Thus, while the plot might have come straight out of Jane Austen, the treatment of the plot is wholly different from anything Jane Austen could have conceived. Which is another way of saying that there is some disparity between what the plot appears to be and what it really is. The rattle of teacups—and the story moves to a large extent in an atmosphere of afternoon tea—is deceptive. When, in the opening paragraph, we are shown Katharine pouring out tea, we are explicitly told that "perhaps a fifth part of her mind was thus occupied." And as most if not all of the characters in the book go through the patterns of social behaviour in which they indulge with only a fifth part of their minds employed in those particular actions, *Night and Day* is not a social comedy—that is, a study of the complications in the relationships of people whose behaviour can be explained generally in terms of the standards of the class to which they belong, with a resolution of those complications prepared for in advance by a certain disposition of probabilities in the pattern of events—but rather a novel of ideas, in which the actions of the chief characters spring not from prejudice or habit but from their own speculations about the nature of reality. "It's life that matters, nothing but life—the process of discovering, the everlasting and perpetual process," says Katharine Hilbery to herself as she walks abstractedly along a London street. Emma Woodhouse could never have said that without rending the fabric of the novel of which she is the heroine.

But to call *Night and Day* a novel of ideas is perhaps misleading; for the action is set against a social background, which is described for its own sake *as* a social background, and the characters are not consistently or universally devices for exploring points of view or illuminat-

21

ing types of consciousness. There are, in fact, three main strata discernible among the characters. The first stratum includes only Katharine herself: here the characterization is subtle and searching, as though the author were exploring aspects of herself. In the second stratum we find William, Ralph and Mary Datchet: here the characterization, while careful and often detailed, is on broader lines and concerned more with illuminating general distinctions between different attitudes and different types of personality than with complete psychological analysis. The third level includes Katharine's parents and Cassandra Otway, where the characters represent simply social or intellectual types, or both; vividly enough done, but without real individualization, so that they don't belong necessarily and only to this story but might be fitted in anywhere. Any other characters are merely slightly suggested types whose function is to precipitate action or produce conversation or trains of thought in the principals. The same general differences are observable in the characterization of *The Voyage Out*.

Is *Night and Day*, then, a novel of ideas masquerading as a social comedy? Is it a confusion of kinds? If not, what new unity emerges from the work as a whole, and if so what qualities does the novel possess which help to atone for this confusion? On the whole, it can be answered without injustice that the novel is a confusion of kinds, but how it comes to be so, and just what its peculiar qualities are, demand some further consideration.

In writing *Night and Day* Virginia Woolf is still sufficiently traditional in her technique to use certain external symbols as devices for indicating the ebb and flow of the plot pattern. Thus a temporary adjustment of relations between a man and a woman is indicated by their becoming engaged, and a breakdown in that adjustment by the engagement's being broken off. The intrusion of a new personality into a group relationship is made clear by the realignment of the marital prospects of that group. The conflict between social confidence and the lack of it is given objective substance by making the two parties to that conflict come from different social classes. To use a term that Virginia Woolf was to use later in criticizing her fellow novelists, the symbols are all materialist. In criticizing Bennett and Wells and Galsworthy, Virginia Woolf said, very shortly after completing *Night and Day*, . . . "for us at this moment the form of fiction most in vogue more often misses than secures the thing we seek. Whether we call it life or spirit, truth or reality, this, the essential thing, has moved off, or on, and refuses to be contained any longer in such ill-fitting vestments as we provide. Nevertheless," she continued, "we go on perseveringly, conscientiously, constructing our two and thirty chapters after a design which more and more ceases to resemble the vision in our minds." [1]

This sounds like criticism of her own earlier novels as well as of her contemporaries. The four and thirty chapters of *Night and Day* provide vestments which do not altogether fit the "life or spirit, truth or reality" which Virginia Woolf was endeavouring to express. We have suggested that the book is a novel of ideas masquerading as a social comedy. It is a novel of ideas in the sense that the

[1] "Modern Fiction." *The Common Reader*, New York, 1925, p. 211. (The essay on "Modern Fiction" is dated April, 1919.)

author seems to be aiming at the exploration and expression of conceptions about the human personality and its behaviour: these conceptions are developed and presented through the plot, through the way in which the characters respond to experience. The interest of the book lies not in the experiences through which the characters pass, but in the ideas generated in them as a result of those experiences, in their mental reactions to events. Devices to force the action into objective patterns (separation, reunion; falling in or out of love) are thus arbitrarily and not necessarily connected with the flow of ideas and mental responses which constitute the novel's main interest. The real plot pattern, in fact, does not depend on the apparent plot pattern, and the fluctuations in the sex relationships of the characters provide a mechanical framework of action on which the pattern of ideas and states of consciousness, which is the essential novel, do not really depend. Chronology is the apparent but not the real disposer of the pattern. With the knowledge of her future development available to him, the critic can see that Virginia Woolf was bound to move away from dependence on a chronological sequence of events. Katharine Hilbery does not require to be pushed in and out of love with a couple of disparate male characters in order that those variations in her mental state in which her creator is chiefly interested can be presented; and the same holds good of the other characters. The same result could be achieved more economically and more effectively by finding devices that would enable the author to turn her characters slowly round, as it were, rather than push them forward in a straight line. The chronological straight line, accepted so

24

far by Virginia Woolf from tradition, was soon to be abandoned in favour of other techniques.

And yet, perhaps, the suggestion that *Night and Day* is in any sense a novel of ideas is misleading, for on a more attentive perusal the reader discovers that its basic interest derives from the fact that Virginia Woolf is as much interested in the emotional context that gives rise to the ideas as in the ideas themselves. She is particularly interested in those states of consciousness where thought and emotion are inextricably mixed. At this period in her development she still seems to feel that the more intelligent she makes the character the more communicable such states of consciousness in the character can be made. (This view was later modified: Mrs. Dalloway has not Katharine Hilbery's intelligence, though she is a sensitive and by no means a stupid woman.)

Quiet as the room was, and undisturbed by the sounds of the present moment, Katharine could fancy that here was a deep pool of past time, and that she and her mother were bathed in the light of sixty years ago. What could the present give, she wondered, to compare with the rich crowd of gifts bestowed by the past? Here was a Thursday morning in process of manufacture; each second was minted fresh by the clock upon the mantelpiece.

In a passage such as this we see that characteristic interest in a state of mind which is at once emotional and speculative. The stillness of the room flows round Katharine to produce a certain awareness of subtle problems of space and time; yet the problems are not inquired into as problems, but merely accepted as indicative of a mood. "Life," said Virginia Woolf in that same essay on modern fiction from which we have already quoted, "is not a series

25

of gig-lamps symmetrically arranged; but a luminous halo, a semi-transparent envelope surrounding us from the beginning of consciousness to the end. Is it not the task of the novelist to convey this varying, this unknown and uncircumscribed spirit, whatever aberration or complexity it may display, with as little mixture of the alien and external as possible? We are not pleading merely for courage and sincerity; we are suggesting that the proper stuff of fiction is a little other than custom would have us believe it."

These remarks, written in April, 1919, (the year in which *Night and Day* was published) make it clear that in writing this novel, or perhaps as an immediate result of writing it, Virginia Woolf was already regarding herself as a rebel against the accepted conventions of fiction writing. She was endeavouring to come closer to "life or spirit, truth or reality" than these conventions would permit. She singles out James Joyce, whose *Ulysses* was then appearing in instalments in the *Little Review,* as one who deserved credit for making, as she wished to make, the "attempt to come closer to life" even if this involved discarding "most of the conventions that are commonly observed by the novelist." "Let us record the atoms as they fall upon the mind in the order in which they fall, let us trace the pattern, however disconnected and incoherent in appearance, which each sight or incident scores upon the consciousness. Let us not take it for granted that life exists more fully in what is commonly thought big than in what is commonly thought small."

In a sense, then, Virginia Woolf is aiming at more realism; for reality to her is "spiritual" rather than "material"; it does not consist in the objective incidents in which the

characters are caught up, but in the pattern of consciousness which follows a path that is only partially dependent
on the chronological sequence of external events. Wells,
Bennett and Galsworthy, she insists, are "materialists,"
and in contrast to them Joyce is "spiritual; he is concerned
at all costs to reveal the flickerings of that innermost flame
which flashes its message through the brain, and in order
to preserve it he disregards with complete courage whatever seems to him adventitious, whether it be probability,
or coherence or any other of these signposts which for generations have served to support the imagination of a reader
when called upon to imagine what he can neither touch
nor see."

Whether this is an accurate diagnosis of Joyce's position
is open to question, but there can be little doubt that it is
a faithful account of her own. Speculation concerning the
nature of reality is doubtless a philosophic rather than a
literary activity, but in Virginia Woolf's case it has literary
implications—implications for the content and structure
of fiction—which require examination.

There are certain typical exaggerations in the history of
literary theory and practice in the light of which whole
literary movements, or at least certain views and methods,
can usefully be seen. One might, for example, consider the
interplay of diverse human emotions as the most "real"
aspect of human life, and construct novels or plays out of
purely emotional patterns. We might call such an exag-
geration the sentimental fallacy, which does not mean that
the works produced by it are necessarily bad, but simply
that they take their origin from a view of human nature
which puts emotional states highest on the stepladder of

27

"real" facts about men and women. This would be true of a certain amount of eighteenth century sentimental literature, and it is true, also, of many minor Jacobean plays. (*'Tis Pity She's a Whore* is a good case in point: here the plot pattern is completed by a moral *emotion* which resolves all conflicts, while no intellectual analysis of the situation is presented at all.) The sentimental fallacy is commoner in drama than in fiction, for the appeal from the stage to a group audience is in the nature of things more dependent on such comparatively unsubtle and unintellectual devices. Its opposite is what we might call the intellectual fallacy, where the most "real" facts about men and women are considered to be their states of mind rather than of heart, and even emotions are presented as making themselves felt intellectually, as trains of thought, as the play of memory connecting similar situations from different periods of time or the answering of certain questions about the nature of life in this way rather than that.

If Virginia Woolf, at this stage in her career, can be considered as an example of the intellectual fallacy, this means, not that her novels are necessarily over intellectual, but that she is most successful in dealing with that class of people who respond to experience by speculation rather than by simple expansion of feeling. Consciousness as she presents it is always meditative, and a train of thought is always for her the best symbol of a state of mind. Here, for example, is her description of Katharine Hilbery at that critical period when Cassandra and William have fallen in love and she has not yet committed herself to marry Ralph:

In truth, now that her mother was away, Katharine did feel less sensible than usual, but as she argued it to herself, there was much less need for sense. Secretly, she was a little shaken by the evidence which the morning had supplied of her immense capacity for—what could one call it?—rambling over an infinite variety of thoughts that were too foolish to be named. She was, for example, walking down a road in Northumberland in the August sunset; at the inn she left her companion, who was Ralph Denham, and was transported, not so much by her own feet as by some invisible means, to the top of a high hill. Here the scents, the sounds among the dry heather-roots, the grass-blades pressed upon the palm of her hand, were all so perceptible that she could experience each one separately. After this her mind made excursions into the dark of the air, or settled upon the surface of the sea, which could be discovered over there, or with equal unreason it returned to its couch of bracken beneath the stars of midnight, and visited the snow valleys of the moon. These fancies would have been in no way strange, since the walls of every mind are decorated with some such tracery, but she found herself suddenly pursuing such thoughts with an extreme ardour, which became a desire to change her actual condition for something matching the conditions of her dream.

Katharine's mind is filled with a series of images, which Virginia Woolf prefers to consider as trains of thought. ("But she found herself suddenly pursuing such thoughts with an extreme ardour, which became a desire to change her actual condition.") This passage, we may note, represents an old-fashioned technique if put beside the accounts of states of consciousness in any of her later novels. It is the traditional method of reporting a state of mind as if articulated, with none of those short cuts and rapid transitions which we find, for example, in *Mrs. Dalloway*. Nor does Virginia Woolf yet feel that necessity of freeing

29

herself from strict chronological sequence that was so important for her later.

That Virginia Woolf is guilty of the intellectual fallacy (perhaps the most respectable of literary habits, and certainly preferable, in a novelist if not in a dramatist, to the sentimental fallacy) she is not for that reason austere in expression or lacking in sensitivity. She uses the statement of ideas in her novels not propositionally, to carry on a chain of reasoning, but with an extreme flexibility, as a means of building up atmosphere, creating a mood, or setting a tone. And she frequently is at pains to paint with great subtlety the physical setting in which the character does his meditating. In *Night and Day* the prevailing setting is that of a darkening winter afternoon (although the story, beginning in autumn, carries the events on until the following summer). Her winter interiors and street scenes represent some of the best writing in the book:

The afternoon light was almost over, and steady streams of greenish and yellowish artificial light were being poured into an atmosphere which, in country lanes, would now have been soft with the smoke of wood fires; and on both sides of the road the shop windows were full of sparkling chains and highly polished leather cases, which stood upon shelves made of thick plate-glass.

What Virginia Woolf selects for description, in a landscape or an interior, is always what will serve as best commentary on or instigator of a state of mind:

A turn of the street, a firelit room, something monumental in the procession of the lamp-posts, who shall say what accident of light or shape had suddenly changed the prospect within his mind . . .

His mind then began to wander about the house, and he wondered whether there were other rooms like the drawing-room, and he thought, inconsequently, how beautiful the bathrooms must be, and how leisurely it was—the life of these well-kept people, who were, no doubt, still sitting in the same room, only they had changed their clothes, and little Mr. Anning was there, and the aunt who would mind if the glass of her father's picture was broken. . . .

Never are voices so beautiful as on a winter's evening, when dusk almost hides the body, and they seem to issue from nothingness with a note of intimacy seldom heard by day. Such an edge was there in Mary's voice when she greeted him. About her seemed to hang the mist of the winter hedges, and the clear red of the bramble leaves. He felt himself at once stepping on to the firm ground of an entirely different world, but he did not allow himself to yield to the pleasure of it directly. . . . In front of them the sky now showed itself of a reddish-yellow, like a slice of some semilucent stone behind which a lamp burnt, while a fringe of black trees with distinct branches stood against the light, which was obscured in one direction by a hump of earth, in all other directions the land lying flat to the very verge of the sky. . . . Mary had gone this walk many hundred times in the course of her life, generally alone, and at different stages the ghosts of past moods would flood her mind with a whole scene or train of thought merely at the sight of three trees from a particular angle, or at the sound of the pheasant clucking in the ditch.

Virginia Woolf uses scenery in order to help break down barriers between thoughts and events, between incidents and emotions and speculations and memories, so that the "semi-transparent envelope surrounding us from the beginning of consciousness to the end" may be presented to the reader. And though on occasions, throughout *Night and Day*, we come across passages which might have come straight out of Jane Austen, we know that these do not represent the real stuff of the novel, but are interludes merely, bridges connecting one attempt to present the semi-transparent envelope and the next. Consider the following, for example:

'My dear,' Cassandra exclaimed, shaking the book at her cousin, 'my whole life's changed from this moment! I must write the man's name down at once, or I shall forget—'

Whose name, what book, which life was changed Katharine proceeded to ascertain. She began to lay aside her clothes hurriedly, for she was very late.

'May I sit and watch you?' Cassandra asked, shutting up her book. 'I got ready on purpose.'

'Oh, you're ready, are you?' said Katharine, half turning in the midst of her operations, and looking at Cassandra, who sat, clasping her knees, on the edge of the bed.

'There are people dining here,' she said, taking in the effect of Cassandra from a new point of view. . . .

'Who's coming to dinner?' Cassandra asked, anticipating further possibilities of rapture.

'There's William, and, I believe, Aunt Eleanor and Uncle Aubrey.'

'I'm so glad William is coming. Did he tell you that he sent me his manuscript? I think it's wonderful— I think he's almost good enough for you, Katharine.'

'You shall sit next to him and tell him what you think of him.'

'I shan't dare do that,' Cassandra asserted.

'Why? You're not afraid of him, are you?'

'A little—because he's connected with you.'

Katharine smiled.

'But then, with your well-known fidelity, considering that you're staying here at least a fortnight, you won't have any illusions left about me by the time you go. I give you a week, Cassandra. I shall see my power fading day by day. Now it's at the climax; but tomorrow it'll have begun to fade. What am I to wear I wonder? Find me a blue dress, Cassandra, over there in the long wardrobe.'

The social comedy provides simply the framework over which the luminous halo is stretched. A passage such as this belongs to the Jane Austen kind of novel that *Night and Day* would have been if its author had been content with what she called "materialism." It is clear that Virginia Woolf had not yet discovered a technique which would enable her to write a novel in which luminous halo and actual story would be coextensive. Both in *The Voyage Out* and *Night and Day* there is, on a fairly superficial level, a simple story whose function is to provide opportunities for the careful presentation of moods and states of mind. The real "plot" of the novel seems to fall between two stools: it is completely developed neither on the "material" nor on the "spiritual" level, and thus the real structure and unity of the book is never completely clear. To resolve on the "spiritual" level a conflict raised on the "material" is not the most effective art, as Virginia Woolf herself seems to have seen after writing *Night and Day*. For she immediately turned to the elaboration of a technique that would enable her to solve this problem.

3. EXPERIMENT AND TRANSITION

IN AN ESSAY ENTITLED "NOTES ON AN ELIZABETHAN PLAY"
Virginia Woolf discusses the difference between "the
Elizabethan view of reality and our own." The reality of
the modern poets and novelists "is, speaking roughly,
based upon the life and death of some knight called Smith,
who succeeded his father in the family business of pit-
wood importers, timber merchants and coal exporters, was
well known in political, temperance and church circles,
did much for the poor of Liverpool, and died last Wednes-
day of pneumonia while on a visit to his son at Muswell
Hill." [1] But when we turn to an Elizabethan play—"Where
is Smith, we ask, where is Liverpool?" The Elizabethan
play sets us free "to wander . . . among dukes and gran-
dees, Gonzaloes and Bellimperias, who spend their lives
in murder and intrigue, dress up as men if they are women,
as women if they are men, see ghosts, run mad, and die in
the greatest profusion on the slightest provocation, utter-

[1] *The Common Reader,* New York, 1925, p. 74.

ing as they fall imprecations of superb vigour or elegies of the wildest despair."

Which, she proceeds to ask, is "reality?" Not the Elizabethan wonderland, which for long stretches at a time is "intolerably dull," nor yet the account of the man whose name was Smith and who lived in Liverpool. But literature that tries to express reality "must somehow be based on Smith, have one toe touching Liverpool, take off into whatever heights it pleases from reality." And she concludes that "there is a station, somewhere in mid-air, whence Smith and Liverpool can be seen to the best advantage; . . . the great artist is the man who knows where to place himself above the shifting scenery."

This problem of discovering and presenting "reality" is at once philosophical and aesthetic: it has implications for epistemology and for the technique of fiction. The writer of fiction, it would seem, has first to answer the question of what reality is and then devise a technique that can express reality in language. But there is no attempt at objectivity in defining the real: though in its discovery the mind plays a part equally with the sensibility, reality emerges as something very different from what can be communicated by a series of propositions. It is a flux, whose essence can best be seized upon by the individual personality acting *as* a personality, not impersonally with mathematical objectivity.

If, then, as Virginia Woolf came to consider, "reality" for the novelist is something the knowledge of which depends on the writer's "station, somewhere in mid-air," the writer of fiction is faced with the problem both of finding that station and, when he has done this, of adequately communicating what he sees from that vantage point.

It comes, indeed, down to this: that "reality" for the novelist is, in a phrase which Virginia Woolf uses in the same essay, determined by "the inexhaustible richness of human sensibility." There is an essential subjectivity here, an interpretation of reality in terms of human reactions, which distinguishes art, one supposes, from science. Prose, Virginia Woolf maintains, is a "lumbering and lagging art" when compared with poetry (and, she would add, with music) because in the latter arts the artist is freed, by the nature of his medium, from the necessity of presenting reality piecemeal, one proposition at a time: poetry can exploit other aspects of language besides the semantic so as to convey the organization of different and even conflicting aspects of a situation simultaneously. Thus a novelist becomes more effective in presenting reality in proportion as his medium approximates to that of the poet. Precedence is not to be ceded to poetry altogether, however, for it requires prose to ensure that the writer "has one toe touching Liverpool." Grounded in prose, the novelist must lean as far towards poetry as is consistent with his maintaining contact with the earth. In this state of unstable equilibrium he is best fitted to communicate a sense of reality.

In the novel as traditionally written in the nineteenth century and the first part of the twentieth, Virginia Woolf saw a form of literature whose normal methods and techniques encouraged the writer to restrict reality wholly to Smith and Liverpool. If this kind of art was accomplished with sufficient skill and cunning, if the novelist's observation of these material events was clear and honest and precise, if his prose was finely chiselled and adequately responsive to the events it was describing, and, above all, if the writer was unpretentious enough to understand that he was writing about Smith and Liverpool and not about the eternal verities—then one might get excellent fiction, excellent, yet limited. Thus Jane Austen is admitted to be a fine novelist: "she knew exactly what her powers were, and what material they were fitted to deal with as material should be dealt with by a writer. . . . There were impressions which lay outside her province; emotions that by no stretch or artifice could be properly coated and covered by her own resources." [1] If the novelist, however, talks of Smith and Liverpool and endeavours to present this as some profound vision of reality, his work—Galsworthy's, for example, and Arnold Bennett's—is reproved as unsatisfactory.

And even Jane Austen, Virginia Woolf suggests, suffers from her limitation of vision. Virginia Woolf speculates on what Jane Austen could have written had she lived to develop her powers further, had she survived a few years more to come out of her obscurity and "stayed in London, dined out, lunched out, met famous people, made new friends, read, travelled, and carried back to the quiet country cottage a hoard of observations to feast upon at leisure." Then Jane Austen would have discovered a deeper vision. "She would have devised a method, clear and composed as ever, but deeper and more suggestive, for conveying not only what people say, but what they leave unsaid; not only what they are, but what life is. She would have stood farther away from her characters, and

[1] *The Common Reader,* p. 202.

seen them more as a group, less as individuals. Her satire, while it played less incessantly, would have been more stringent and severe. She would have been the forerunner of Henry James and Proust. . . ." She might have added, the forerunner of Virginia Woolf.

It is clear that Virginia Woolf is concerned here with the same contrast as that which disturbed her in her essay on an Elizabethan play and her account of Galsworthy, Bennett and Wells—the contrast between events patterned and recorded objectively, as by the interested observer who, standing at the same level as his characters, looks and listens and notes down and arranges what he sees and hears, and events patterned and recorded by one who is seeking "reality," one who mingles impressions and mood and atmosphere, who abandons propositional statements and strict chronology in order to weave a speculative texture that is a symbol of "what life is."

The older writers might have replied that both they and their readers were well aware of what life was, and it was not the business of a writer of fiction to repeat truths which religion or philosophy had already formulated. Accepting these truths, taking them for granted, they would construct a pattern of imaginary events over against them. Their function was not to investigate reality, but to formulate impressive examples of human behaviour, always assuming that reality to exist. And in making this reply they would have laid their finger on the chief difference between their objective and that of Virginia Woolf.

For Virginia Woolf, unlike Jane Austen, was writing in a world in which there was no concensus of opinion concerning what "reality" was, and, unlike some of her contemporaries, she was very much aware of that lack of agreement. The second and third decades of the twentieth century, which saw Virginia Woolf's flowering as a novelist, saw also the final dissolution of that common background of belief and attitude that made it possible for a writer to talk of Smith and Liverpool while assuming certain unarticulated preconceptions concerning the nature and value of human life which made communication on what Virginia Woolf called the "materialist" level at the same time statements about "reality." Virginia Woolf had, as it were, to start from scratch, to provide each character with a world view in the light of which it was to be interpreted. The events recorded in her novels were not acted out against a solid background of belief, a stable emotional and intellectual pattern: they had, on the contrary, to be invested with their own philosophic and emotional background. Virginia Woolf had come face to face with the problem that challenged so many of her contemporary artists, the problem of producing significant art in an individualistic and sceptical age.

Art without belief—without, that is, community belief—is not easy to create. For here the artist has to throw his own sensibility around each work in such a way as to provide the reader or beholder with a philosophic background sufficient to serve as a key to the patterning of that particular work. As that key is no longer provided by the civilization in which both writer and reader live, it is up to the writer to provide one himself. Virginia Woolf has, therefore, to find a method of writing which enables her to tell a story while at the same time indicating the particular view of "reality" which gives that story significance.

39

This is the explanation of her constant concern with "reality."

Virginia Woolf was more aware of the nature of the situation than other writers who reacted to it similarly, but less consciously. In an essay entitled "How It Strikes a Contemporary" she discusses this very point, the relation of art to community belief. Referring to the "sense of security" that emerges from the work of Wordsworth, Scott and Jane Austen, she asks, "From what, then, arises that sense of security which gradually, delightfully, and completely overcomes us?" And her reply is worth noting: "It is the power of their belief—their conviction, that imposes itself upon us. . . . They have their judgment of conduct. They know the relations of human beings towards each other and towards the universe. Neither of them [Jane Austen and Scott] probably has a word to say about the matter outright, but everything depends on it. . . . To believe that your impressions hold good for others is to be released from the cramp and confinement of personality." [1]

And this is precisely the point. The moderns, as Virginia Woolf saw them, lived in an age without common belief and therefore could not be free from the cramp and confinement of personality. "Our contemporaries afflict us because they have ceased to believe," she complains in the same essay. Yet there was a way out of the difficulty. It might be possible to make a virtue of necessity, to find a way of writing which would call for dependence on the writer's personality, a way of writing out of a personal sense of truth so as to convey that sense to the reader as

[1] *The Common Reader,* pp. 328–29.

he reads. That is the course that Virginia Woolf took.[1]

Whether an age is without belief or not can never, perhaps, be objectively determined. The point is that Virginia Woolf considered it to be so, and formulated her literary position accordingly.[2] Among her contemporaries there were certain sensitive and responsive individuals who looked on the problem of art as she did, who saw, however indirectly or subconsciously, the necessity of compensating by something within the work itself for the lack of a background common to reader and writer. There were other writers who were not conscious of that necessity, and continued to assume the existence of a background which may or may not have actually existed. It is at this point that the question of "which audience?" comes up. Suburban Manchester may have continued throughout

[1] "What is meant by reality?" asked Virginia Woolf in a lecture at Cambridge in 1928. And she answered: "It would seem to be something very erratic, very undependable—now to be found in a dusty road, now in a scrap of newspaper in the street, now in a daffodil in the sun. It lights up a group in a room and stamps some casual saying. It overwhelms one walking home beneath the stars and makes the silent world more real than the world of speech—and then there it is again in an omnibus in the uproar of Piccadilly. Sometimes, too, it seems to dwell in shapes too far away for us to discern what their nature is. But whatever it touches, it fixes and makes permanent. That is what remains over when the skin of the day has been cast into the hedge; that is what is left of past time and of our loves and hates. Now the writer, as I think, has the chance to live more than other people in the presence of this reality. It is his business to find it and collect it and communicate it to the rest of us." *A Room of One's Own,* New York, 1929, pp. 191–92.

[2] "At the present moment we are suffering, not from decay, but from having no code of manners which writers and readers accept as a prelude to the more exciting intercourse of friendship." *Mr. Bennett and Mrs. Brown,* London, 1928, p. 21.

this period in the same general frame of mind as the Victorians possessed, but Bloomsbury certainly did not. There can be no doubt that that particular class of urban intellectual to which Virginia Woolf all her life belonged (and we must not forget Leslie Stephen, and the kind of upbringing his daughter would have had) looked for the meaning of life in the sensibility of the individual. ("Sensibility" referring not to an emotional state, but to a complex of thoughts and feelings in which the intellectual element tended to be dominant.)

In *The Voyage Out* and *Night and Day* Virginia Woolf tried to achieve this anchoring of the story in a particular scheme of value or view of "reality" by conscious argument and reflection on the part of the characters, and the result was that both books have a certain heaviness and over-intellectualization which the sensitive reader resents. She then attempted to discover a medium and a technique which would enable her to achieve the same end more economically and more effectively—a prose style that would enable her to utilize some of the resources of poetry in creating a view of life as the story moved, and a structure that would enable her to transcend the traditional limitations of narrative and construct a meditative web of retrospect, anticipation and analogy that would build up atmosphere and interpret life as the novel proceeded.

The creation of what, at the risk of appearing pedantic, we shall call an "interpretative atmosphere" became, then, the goal of Virginia Woolf's art. She wanted to find a way of writing which would interpret events as it described them, show both the thing and its value, its metaphysical meaning, simultaneously. And so she turned aside from writing complete novels to experiment. The sketches that she collected in 1921 under the title *Monday or Tuesday* are the record of this experimentation.

All this is not to say that Virginia Woolf, impelled by something in the "intellectual climate" of her time, or by the "spirit of the age," gravitated inevitably towards this kind of writing. That her own type of sensibility had been guiding her in this direction from the beginning is evident from her earliest work, and the qualities of mind that she displayed in *The Voyage Out* and *Night and Day* give some indication of the way she was to go. Estimates of causes in the world of art can at best be suggestions, adumbrations, hints at illuminating comparisons or parallels. Neither psychology nor sociology can fully explain either the development of literature in general nor the course taken by a particular writer; yet each provides certain insights which no critic would willingly do without. For a novel, even if considered in complete isolation as a "work of art," requires to be looked at in proper perspective if its organization is to be properly understood. The question of the "aesthetic distance" at which the reader ought to stand in order to see the essential work is one that can rarely be answered without reference to some background material.

Having said this, in an effort to avoid misunderstanding, we may return to a discussion of *Monday or Tuesday*. This is a collection of eight short sketches, written in 1919 and 1920, [1] which show Virginia Woolf experimenting with prose, trying to develop a more fluid medium, a medium

[1] Two of them, *The Mark on the Wall* and *Kew Gardens,* were first published separately in 1919.

more suited to the expression of that "luminous halo" which for her was reality. They were gropings towards the method she would have to employ in writing fiction if she was to be successful in conveying to the reader as she wrote her own personal sense of reality.

The opening piece, "A Haunted House," is simply an exercise in the writing of fluid, associative prose. There is here a deliberate attempt to transcend the limits of formal prose statement by using mental or emotional association as an excuse for keeping the narrative flexible to the point where sequence and chronology cease to be important. The organizing factor is simply the writer's mood, not the pattern of a story: time and space shift at will while the mood remains constant, in contrast to more traditional narrative, in which the events march steadily forward, solidly grounded in space and spread out chronologically in time, and the mood depends on the events. The sketch is simply a study in impressionism, and is no more a finished work than a painter's preliminary study of a hand or an arm is a finished portrait. The manner in which the images revolve round the central mood is illustrated by the following quotation:

But they had found it in the drawing room. Not that one could ever see them. The window panes reflected apples, reflected roses; all the leaves were green in the grass. If they moved in the drawing room, the apple only turned its yellow side. Yet, the moment after, if the door was opened, spread about the floor, hung upon the walls, pendant from the ceiling—what? My hands were empty. The shadow of a thrush crossed the carpet; from the deepest wells of silence the wood pigeon drew its bubble of sound. "Safe, safe, safe," the pulse of the house beat softly. "The treasure buried; the room . . ." the pulse stopped short. Oh, was that the buried treasure?

44

A moment later the light had faded. Out in the garden then? But the trees spun darkness for a wandering beam of sun. So fine, so rare, coolly sunk beneath the surface the beam I sought always burnt behind the glass. Death was the glass; death was between us; coming to the woman first, hundreds of years ago, leaving the house, sealing all the windows; the rooms were darkened. He left it, left her, went North, went East, saw the stars turned in the Southern sky; sought the house, found it dropped beneath the Downs. "Safe, safe, safe," the pulse of the house beat gladly. "The Treasure yours."

The next piece, the longest in the book, is entitled "A Society," and differs considerably from the others in this collection. For here a similar type of prose is employed for a satiric purpose. The writing is less fluid, the narrative thread is more distinct, than it is in "A Haunted House," and though the events and images are all symbolic there is less abandonment to impressionism. One might call the sketch a parable, with a core of narrative more luminous and less definable than in most parables. There is also a note of high spiritedness and exuberance which, together with the other features of "A Society" make us recognize in it a precursor of that curious and exciting *tour de force* that Virginia Woolf produced some years later and which is discussed in another chapter—*Orlando*. Briefly, the narrative is concerned with a group of young women who, over a period of five years, devote themselves to an investigation of the way men are running civilization, determined to satisfy themselves that men are fulfilling the great aim of "producing good people and good books" before consenting to take up their duties as wives and mothers. The investigation is inconclusive, and one of the investigators falls in love and has a baby before it is at an

45

end. But such a summary does not do justice to "A Society," which bristles throughout with humorous irony expressed through a most effective symbolism:

Off we went, then, some to the British Museum; others to the King's Navy; some to Oxford; others to Cambridge; we visited the Royal Academy and the Tate; heard modern music in concert rooms, went to the Law Courts, and saw new plays. No one dined out without asking her partner certain questions and carefully noting his replies. At intervals we met together and compared our observations. Oh, those were merry meetings! Never have I laughed so much as I did when Rose read her notes upon "Honour" and described how she had dressed herself as an Æthiopian Prince and gone aboard one of His Majesty's ships. Discovering the hoax, the Captain visited her (now disguised as a private gentleman) and demanded that honour should be satisfied. "But how?" she asked. "How?" he bellowed. "With the cane of course!" Seeing that he was beside himself with rage and expecting that her last moment had come, she bent over and received, to her amazement, six light taps upon the behind. "The honour of the British Navy is avenged!" he cried, and, raising herself, she saw him with the sweat pouring down his face holding out a trembling right hand. "Away!" she exclaimed, striking an attitude and imitating the ferocity of his own expression, "My honour has still to be satisfied!" "Spoken like a gentleman!" he returned, and fell into profound thought. "If six strokes avenge the honour of the King's Navy," he mused, "how many avenge the honour of a private gentleman?" . . . "Let me see," he cried suddenly, "did your father keep a carriage?" "No," she said. "Or a riding horse?" "We had a donkey," she bethought her, "which drew the mowing machine." At this his face lighted. "My mother's name—" she added. "For God's sake, man, don't mention your mother's name!" he shrieked, trembling like an aspen and flushing to the roots of his hair, and it was ten minutes at least before she could induce him to proceed. At length he decreed that if she gave him four strokes and a half in the small of the back at a spot indicated by himself (the half conceded, he said, in recognition of the fact that her great grandmother's uncle was killed at Trafalgar) it was his opinion that her honour would be as good as new. This was done; they retired to a restaurant; drank two bottles of wine for which he insisted upon paying; and parted with protestations of eternal friendship.

The slight touch of buffoonery prevents this sketch from being merely a parable: the mood of ironical criticism includes even the critic.

Elizabeth rose and said that in order to prosecute her inquiry she had dressed as a man and been taken for a reviewer.

"I have read new books pretty steadily for the past five years," said she. "Mr. Wells is the most popular living writer; then comes Mr. Arnold Bennett; then Mr. Compton Mackenzie; Mr. McKenna and Mr. Walpole may be bracketed together.

. . . "But," we pressed her, "do they write good books?"

"Good books?" she said, looking at the ceiling. "You must remember," she began, speaking with extreme rapidity, "that fiction is the mirror of life. And you can't deny that education is of the highest importance, and that it would be extremely annoying, if you found yourself alone at Brighton late at night, not to know which was the best boarding house to stay at, and suppose it was a dripping Sunday evening—wouldn't it be nice to go to the Movies?"

"But what has that got to do with it?" we asked.

"Nothing—nothing—nothing whatever," she replied.

"Well, tell us the truth," we bade her.

"The truth? But isn't it wonderful," she broke off— "Mr. Chitter has written a weekly article for the past thirty years upon love or hot buttered toast and has sent all his sons to Eton—"

"The truth!" we demanded.

"Oh, the truth," she stammered, "the truth has nothing to do with literature," and sitting down she refused to say another word.

It all seemed to us very inconclusive.

The title piece, a brief sketch of two short pages, is perhaps the least successful of any in the book. It is simply an exercise in the communication of a shifting mood through associated images, but the images shift so rapidly that no mood communicates itself. And intellect keeps interfering with the images.

> Desiring truth, awaiting it, laboriously distilling a few words, for ever desiring—(a cry starts to the left, another to the right. Wheels strike divergently. Omnibuses conglomerate in conflict)—for ever desiring—(the clock asseverates with twelve distinct strokes that it is midday; light sheds gold scales; children swarm) —for ever desiring truth. Red is the dome; coins hang on the trees; smoke trails from the chimneys; bark, shout, cry "Iron for sale"—and truth?

The sketch that follows, "An Unwritten Novel," is a study in the presentation of character through the juxtaposition of symbolic imagery, with an ironical conclusion. Here images and speculations are organized into an illustration not of life but its quality, its mood; and the conclusion (in which the real circumstances of the character's life turn out to be altogether different from the images and meditations which the author had employed to make the characterization) illustrates, with ironical humour, the dangers run by novelists who see the lives of others through their own sensibility. The situation is simple: the author, sitting opposite a woman in the train, constructs in her mind what she considers an appropriate past and appropriate connections for the character; and what she sees when the woman reaches her destination and leaves the train contradicts all this imagined background.

There follows a short sketch entitled "The String Quartet," which is again an experiment with the raw material of fiction. Virginia Woolf is here attempting to give an impression of a concert at which a Mozart quartet is played, the impression, first, of the scattered chatter throughout the hall before the music starts; then of the music itself, allegro, slow movement, and lively finale; and lastly of the conclusion, and the departure of the audience. The main characteristic of the technique here is the elimination of all conventional transitions and the attempt to present the whole experience as a continuous flow. Disparate fragments of conversation worked into a single stream of talk; and then the music rendered in a series of impressionistic images:

Flourish, spring, burgeon, burst! The pear tree on the top of the mountain. Fountains jet; drops descend. But the waters of the Rhone flow swift and deep, race under the arches, and sweep the trailing water leaves, washing shadows over the silver fish, the spotted fish rushed down by the swift waters, now swept into an eddy where—it's difficult this—conglomeration of fish all in a pool; leaping, splashing, scraping sharp fins; and such a boil of current that the yellow pebbles are churned round and round, round and round—free now, rushing downwards, or even somehow ascending in exquisite spirals into the air; curled like thin shavings from under a plane; up and up. . . . How lovely goodness is in those who, stepping lightly, go smiling through the world! Also in jolly old fishwives, squatted under arches, obscene old women, how deeply they laugh and shake and rollick, when they walk, from side to side, hum, hah!

The impression of the music is not conveyed solely in a series of images: as one might expect from Virginia Woolf, the intellectual element is there too. In the following extract the number of abstract ideas are about equal to the number of images:

Tramp and trumpeting. Clang and clangour. Firm establishment. Fast foundations. March of myriads. Confusion and chaos trod to earth. But this city to which we travel has neither stone nor marble; hangs enduring; stands unshakable; nor does a face, nor does a flag greet or welcome. Leave then to perish your hope; droop in the desert my joy; naked advance. Bare are the pillars; auspicious to none; casting no shade; resplendent; severe. Back then I fall, eager no more, desiring only to go, find the street, mark the buildings, greet the applewoman, say to the maid who opens the door: A starry night.

The piece that follows is a very short exercise in the impressionistic use of imagery to convey colour. There are two paragraphs, the first entitled simply GREEN and the second BLUE. Here we find a precision of detail in description of symbolic scenes alternating with a more purely intellectual expansion of the reverie, so as to fill out a picture of a flowing mood or atmosphere. The characters which appear are created in order to symbolize and illustrate the mood: the mood, as always in Virginia Woolf, is that of the observer, the author herself, even when it pretends to be that of the character. The technique here is more reminiscent of that of the French Symbolists than anywhere else in Virginia Woolf's writings:

Thrown upon the beach he lies, blunt, obtuse, shedding dry blue scales. Their metallic blue stains the rusty iron on the beach. Blue are the ribs of the wrecked rowing boat. A wave rolls beneath the blue bells. But the cathedral's different, cold, incense laden, faint blue with the veils of madonnas.

A similar method is employed in the next piece, "Kew Gardens," where Virginia Woolf conveys not only the visual impressions of the gardens, but the mood of typical and symbolic characters who haunt them. Again, the author's reverie is what organizes the images and the characters; and an intellectual play uses the images as starting points for meditation. The volume concludes with "The Mark on the Wall," in which, out of a single situation—the author sitting by the fire on a winter evening, noticing on the wall opposite a mark she cannot remember having seen before, which arouses her curiosity—Virginia Woolf weaves a dreamy reverie of images, ideas and reminiscences:

No, no, nothing is proved, nothing is known. And if I were to get up at this very moment and ascertain that the mark on the wall is really—what shall we say?—the head of a gigantic old nail, driven in two hundred years ago, which has now, owing to the patient attrition of many generations of housemaids, revealed its head above the coat of paint, and is taking its first view of modern life in the sight of a white-walled fire-lit room, what should I gain?—Knowledge? Matter for further speculation? I can think sitting still as well as standing up. And what is knowledge? What are our learned men save the descendants of witches and hermits who crouched in caves and in woods brewing herbs, interrogating shrew-mice and writing down the language of the stars? And the less we honour them as our superstitions dwindle and our respect for beauty and health of mind increases. . . . Yes, one could imagine a very pleasant world. A quiet, spacious world, with the flowers so red and blue in the open fields.

At the conclusion, daily life impinges on the reverie:

There is a vast upheaval of matter. Someone is standing over me and saying—
"I'm going out to buy a newspaper."
"Yes?"
"Though it's no good buying newspapers. . . . Nothing ever happens. Curse this war; God damn this war! . . . All the same, I don't see why we should have a snail on our wall."
Ah, the mark on the wall! It was a snail.

This conclusion is particularly interesting, for it shows

51

Virginia Woolf employing a method of moving from reverie to incident—a method, that is, which will enable her
to use this kind of meditative prose in a complete novel.

Monday or Tuesday is a series of literary exercises rather
than of finished works; apart from the arbitrarily chosen
mood of the author, there is no larger pattern in terms of
which the details are chosen or integrated. But the exercises are of great interest to anyone concerned with the
development of Virginia Woolf's technique as a writer of
fiction. All her later works show her utilizing the methods
that she worked out in these sketches, and utilizing them
as means to a larger end, the presentation of a complete
and unified work of fiction. *Monday or Tuesday* marks the
real turning point in Virginia Woolf's career, as is clearly
shown by an examination of the novels that followed.

4. THE SEMI-TRANSPARENT ENVELOPE

AFTER THE EXPERIMENTATION REPRESENTED BY *MONDAY OR Tuesday,* Virginia Woolf was ready to embark on a series of full length novels which would employ the new techniques she had mastered. She had now worked out a style that would enable her to embody in fiction her conception of the flux of experience, a style that was flexible, impressionistic, meditative. The problem to attack next was that of structure and organization: how could such a style be employed in the writing of a novel? *Jacob's Room,* which appeared in 1922, was her first answer to this question.

We have seen why Virginia Woolf was led to abandon the more traditional forms which she had employed in her first two novels. It would be a mistake, however, to regard her development as wholly unrelated to the ideas and techniques of other writers of the time. That she read and was impressed by James Joyce's *Ulysses* we know from her appreciative reference to this work in 1919, when it was appearing in the *Little Review.* And there can be no doubt that the fluidity of Joyce's prose, his avoidance of conventional transitions in his attempt to capture the "stream of consciousness" of his characters, had a permanent effect on Virginia Woolf's style: indeed, some of the experiments in *Monday or Tuesday* were almost certainly suggested by her reading of *Ulysses*. That Marcel Proust, too, whose vast novel sequence she read in the original French in 1922, influenced her subsequent work cannot be doubted. But studies of influences can be overdone: the important thing to realize is that if Virginia Woolf allowed herself to be influenced by Joyce or Proust it was not simply because she happened to have read them, but because she recognized in their achievements something that would help her in accomplishing her own ideal. Joyce's handling of the "monologue intérieur," his presentation of consciousness through the characters' mingled retrospect and anticipation, with the accompanying emancipation from strict chronology; Proust's preoccupation with the quality of experience in time, his Bergsonian sense of duration, his ability to fill and colour the bubble of present time with a vision of the past [1]—these things obviously had their effect on Virginia Woolf, but only because she had already formulated her own aim and was looking for the means of accomplishing it in the completest way. It would be possible, too, to consider the relation of Virginia Woolf's conception of time to Henri Bergson's conception of *durée* or William James's view of the nature of consciousness—but these are considerations which do not

[1] The image is Clive Bell's. Bell's little book on Proust appeared in 1928 and reflected the interest in Proust of the literary and artistic circle in which Virginia Woolf moved. Bell married Virginia Woolf's sister, Vanessa.

in themselves help us to an understanding of her essential aims and methods, and they can be safely left to the future historian of culture or the contemporary student in search of a PH.D. subject.

In *Jacob's Room* that studied tenuousness of expression which was coming to be one of the chief characteristics of Virginia Woolf's style is abundantly evident. There is no attempt here to preserve the firm outlines of chronological events; experience is broken down into a series of rapidly dissolving impressions which merge into one another but which are kept from complete dissolution by the meditative eye of the author, who keeps the flux of things constantly in sight, and preserves her own character sufficiently to be able to comment intermittently on the intangible nature of her subject:

> It seems then that men and women are equally at fault. It seems that a profound, impartial and absolutely just opinion of our fellow-creatures is utterly unknown. Either we are men, or we are women. Either we are cold, or we are sentimental. Either we are young, or growing old. In any case life is but a procession of shadows, and God knows why it is that we embrace them so eagerly, and see them depart with such anguish, being shadows. And why, if this and much more than this is true, why are we yet surprised in the window corner by a sudden vision that the young man in the chair is of all things in the world the most real, the most solid, the best known to us— why indeed? For the moment after we know nothing about him.
>
> Such is the manner of our seeing. Such the conditions of our love.

Or this comment:

> One word is sufficient. But if one cannot find it?

The story opens with a series of pictures of Betty Flanders, widowed mother of three children, on holiday with the children in Cornwall. These pictures are a series of impressions, speculations, images, attitudes, in the course of which the few essential facts that the reader must know to get his bearings in the book are unobtrusively let out one at a time and with an appearance of casualness:

Such were Betty Flanders's letters to Captain Barfoot—many-paged, tear-stained. Scarborough is seven hundred miles from Cornwall: Captain Barfoot is in Scarborough: Seabrook is dead. Tears made all the dahlias in her garden undulate in red waves and flashed the glass house in her eyes, and spangled the kitchen with bright knives, and made Mrs. Jarvis, the rector's wife, think at church, while the hymn-tune played and Mrs. Flanders bent low over her little boys' heads, that marriage is a fortress and widows stray solitary in the open fields, picking up stones, gleaning a few golden straws, unprotected, poor creatures. Mrs. Flanders had been a widow these two years.

The point of view keeps shifting; characters are introduced whose sole function is to have fleeting impressions of the principals, which Virginia Woolf can record. An individual is the sum of his own impressions and those he makes on his fellows, and the character of Jacob, Betty Flanders's youngest son, is thus conveyed by a series of indirect strokes. And sometimes the light is suddenly and briefly thrown on the minor character who is introduced solely to give his impression of a major character—yet not solely, for this sudden flash of light reveals him, too, as an independent person with a life of his own somewhere in the background, with experiences, prejudices, a texture of living. Thus the artist who is introduced for a moment in

56

order that his impression of Betty Flanders on the Cornwall beach might be recorded gets his moment, too:

Here was that woman moving—actually going to get up—confound her! He struck the canvas a hasty violet-black dab. For the landscape needed it. It was too pale—greys flowing into lavenders, and one star or a white gull suspended just so—too pale as usual. The critics would say it was too pale, for he was an unknown man exhibiting obscurely, a favourite with his landladies' children, wearing a cross on his watch chain, and much gratified if his landladies liked his pictures—which they often did.

We get here a searching glimpse into another life, a life which while impinging momentarily on the affairs of the Flanders family has yet a background of its own, which determines the nature of that impingement. Experience is flux, and the lives of different men shade imperceptibly into each other.

The book is organized around Jacob's life—from his childhood, through his student days at Cambridge, to his proud independence in rooms in London, his love affairs, his visit to France and Greece, and then (though this is never directly referred to) his death in the war, leaving only impressions of himself in the minds of others and a room full of his belongings which for a time at least has the power to renew those impressions in those who knew him. The point of view keeps shifting: the experience which Virginia Woolf impressionistically renders belongs now to Jacob, now to his mother, now to any one of a number of his friends or associates. Virginia Woolf passes freely from one to another, the transitions being determined not by any preconceived scale of emphases but by the needs of the moment—the need for indicating the

57

interrelationship of different experiences which makes itself felt, spontaneously it would appear, at intervals
throughout the story. The quality of academic life at
Cambridge—the happy and excited conversation of young
men in comfortable rooms with the light fading; excursions on the river, with all the atmosphere of the Cambridge countryside; the dry self-contained life of dons;
and over all the mellow light of an environment that has
filtered down through antiquity—all this is rendered in a
series of brief pictures which succeed each other without
formal introduction or conclusion, and in a similar way
we are shown Jacob's life in London, his social relationships there, the girls who fall in love with him, the friend-
ships which help to condition the quality of his experience. And we are left in the end with only his room, where
his mother and his friend are going over the belongings of
the now vanished young man. His experiences have rolled
themselves together in past time and been transmuted into
the memories and associations of others:

Listless is the air in an empty room, just swelling the curtain;
the flowers in the jar shift. One fibre in the wicker arm-chair
creaks, though no one sits there.

Bonamy crossed to the window. Pickford's van swung down the
street. The omnibuses were locked together at Mudie's corner.
Engines throbbed, and carters, jamming the brakes down, pulled
their horses sharp up. A harsh and unhappy voice cried something
unintelligible. And then suddenly all the leaves seemed to raise
themselves.

"Jacob! Jacob!" cried Bonamy, standing by the window. The
leaves sank down again.

"Such confusion everywhere!" exclaimed Betty Flanders, burst-
ing open the bedroom door.

Bonamy turned away from the window.

THE SEMI-TRANSPARENT ENVELOPE

> "What am I to do with these, Mr. Bonamy?"
> She held out a pair of Jacob's old shoes.

And so life recedes into time, which holds them all, as Virginia Woolf has been suggesting in various ways throughout the book:

> But their voices floated for a little above the camp. The moonlight destroyed nothing. The moor accepted everything. Tom Gage cries aloud so long as his tombstone endures. The Roman skeletons are in safe keeping. Betty Flanders's darning needles are safe too and her garnet brooch. And sometimes at mid-day, in the sunshine, the moor seems to hoard these little treasures, like a nurse. But at midnight when no one speaks or gallops, and the thorn tree is perfectly still, it would be foolish to vex the moor with questions—what? and why?
> The church clock, however, strikes twelve.

The "however" in this last sentence is worth noting. The apparently rigid divisions of time challenge the fluid unity into which all experience flows.

In rendering impressions of specific scenes throughout *Jacob's Room*, Virginia Woolf makes use of the techniques she had elaborated in *Monday or Tuesday*. Jacob, on an impulse, enters St. Paul's Cathedral:

> Dim it is, haunted by ghosts of white marble, to whom the organ forever chaunts. If a boot creaks, it's awful; then the order; the discipline. The verger with his rod has life ironed out beneath him. Sweet and holy are the angelic choristers. And for ever round the marble shoulders, in and out of the folded fingers, go the thin high sounds of voice and organ. For ever requiem—repose. Tired with scrubbing the steps of the Prudential Society's office, which she did year in year out, Mrs. Lidgett took her seat beneath the great Duke's tomb, folded her hands, and half closed her eyes. A magnificent place for an old woman to rest in, by the very side of the great Duke's bones, whose victories mean nothing to her,

whose name she knows not, though she never fails to greet the little angels opposite, as she passes out, wishing the like on her own tomb, for the leathern curtain of the heart has flapped wide, and out steal on tiptoe thoughts of rest, sweet melodies. . . .

And over all plays the meditative intellect of the author, pondering on life, chewing the cud of experience:

Whether we know what was in his mind is another question. Granted ten years' seniority and a difference of sex, fear of him comes first; this is swallowed up by a desire to help—overwhelming sense, reason, and the time of night; anger would follow close on that—with Florinda, with destiny; and then up would bubble an irresponsible optimism. "Surely there's enough light in the street at this moment to drown all our cares in gold!" Ah, what's the use of saying it? Even while you speak and look over your shoulder towards Shaftesbury Avenue, destiny is chipping a dent in him. He has turned to go. As for following him back to his rooms, no—that we won't do.

There is discernible here a certain lack of confidence on the author's part in her own technique. She has to introduce herself at intervals, *in propria persona,* to explain her doubts and difficulties to the reader, and enlist his sympathy. In her later works this device is found much less often.

The description of Jacob's environment often takes the form of simple word-painting, a collection of images whose symbolic function is indicated by the author's illustrative comment:

The mainland, not so very far off—you could see clefts in the cliffs, white cottages, smoke going up—wore an extraordinary look of calm, of sunny peace, as if wisdom and piety had descended upon the dwellers there. Now a cry sounded, as of a man calling pilchards in a main street. It wore an extraordinary look of piety and peace, as if old men smoked by the door, and girls stood, hands on hips, at the well, and horses stood; as if the end of the world had come, and cabbage fields and stone walls, and coast-guard stations, and, above all, the white sand bays with the waves breaking unseen by any one, rose to heaven in a kind of ecstasy.

It would be possible, but scarcely profitable, to analyse the "plot" of *Jacob's Room*: the book was written for the sake of the impressions, of the fluid rendering of experience—one might say, for the sake of style. The book begins with Jacob's mother collecting her youngsters on the beach, and ends with Jacob's life bequeathing itself, as it were, to his past associates and environments. The interpretation of reality that Virginia Woolf was seeking does not emerge from the relation of the parts to the whole so much as from the individual insights which succeed each other throughout the book. In abandoning certain aspects of the traditional novel technique, Virginia Woolf also abandoned, temporarily, all conception of plot as a means of interpreting reality. In *Jacob's Room* experience is not patterned by plot; plot is simply the by-product of the record of the flow of experience. In her next novel, however, Virginia Woolf introduces a new conception of plot. *Mrs. Dalloway* is much more carefully patterned, and here the significance of the whole is not the sum of the significance of the different parts but depends on the shape and disposition of the completed story.

Mrs. Dalloway, which appeared in 1925, is perhaps the first wholly successful novel that Virginia Woolf produced. In her first two novels the traditional plot structure was not adequate to house the kind of insights into experience that Virginia Woolf intended to communicate in her fiction; *Monday and Tuesday* is simply a series of experimental sketches; *Jacob's Room* shows the author having mastered a new technique for presenting experience and lacking a means of integrating the impressionist renderings of individual experiences into a satisfactory unity. In *Mrs. Dalloway* a deliberate attempt is made both to bring all the tracts of experience explored into a single focus and to effect all transitions from one part to another in such a way that the unity of the work is emphasized rather than (as in *Jacob's Room*) weakened by the continual shifts.

Mrs. Dalloway, the central character in the book, is introduced at the beginning as she goes out to do a morning's shopping for her party the same evening. The book ends with an account of the party. But before the author has reached the end of the novel she has managed to give the reader a full account not only of Mrs. Dalloway's past, her development, her character, her history, but also of the history of a varied group of other persons who are related to her either in that they accidentally cross her path at some moment in the course of the day, or that she thinks of them, or that they think of her, or in virtue of some other kind of relationship. None of these relationships are casual, though at first sight they might seem so. Each character who makes contact with Mrs. Dalloway in space (crossing her path in London), in time (doing something at the same moment that she is), or in memory (the third dimension, as it were) has some symbolic relation if not to Mrs. Dalloway herself then to the main theme of the book, in the interpretation of which the life

62

and character of Mrs. Dalloway plays such an important part. What first appears to be a random cross-section of life on a summer morning in London in 1919 emerges on closer scrutiny as a subtly organized patterning of experience, with each part having some reference to the other, the very reverse of that simple impressionism towards which Virginia Woolf seemed to be turning a few years earlier.

Virginia Woolf's method of developing the story is worth noting. In the first place, she presents the individual "stream of consciousness" as compounded of retrospect and anticipation (anticipation depending on and produced by retrospect, with the present moment simply the flow of one into the other), and by doing this she can follow a character back into his past without expanding the chronological limits of the story beyond the single day which provides the framework of the action. Just as in *Ulysses* Joyce takes a chronological framework of less than twenty-four hours and by probing into the mental states of his characters during that time is able to present to the reader almost the whole of their past history without obviously digressing or holding up the progress of the story, so Virginia Woolf in *Mrs. Dalloway* is able to escape from the limitations of chronology by effective use of the "monologue intérieur." Secondly, she takes the two categories of time and space and uses them in almost regular alternation in order to effect transitions between different situations. Once we have been introduced to a character we remain for some time inside that character's mind, going back and forth in time as the character recalls the past or plans the future. And after we have remained within

63

one character's mind for some time, Virginia Woolf, bringing that character's reverie up to the present moment, reminds the reader of someone else who is pursuing his own train of thought at the same moment. Thus we either stand still in time and move from character to character, or we stand still in space, remaining with one character and moving up and down in time with his consciousness. While we are going up and down in time within the single character's consciousness Virginia Woolf constantly reminds us that this journey through time is taking place within an individual mind by the regular repetition of such phrases as "so it seemed to her," "she could remember," "she thought, walking on"; or by other indications that the reverie belongs to that character, such as value judgments punctuating the reverie—judgments made on the character's behalf by the author, employing neither the pronoun "he" (or "she"), which would indicate the author talking about the character, nor the first personal pronoun "I," which would indicate the character making these judgments dramatically in his own person, but the compromise pronoun "one"—"For Heaven only knows why one loves it so"; "for it was not her one hated, but the idea of her." Thus the unifying factor in these reveries is the personality of the individual who indulges in them, which is why Virginia Woolf keeps reminding us of this personality by these interruptions. And when she leaves the character whose stream of consciousness she has been presenting, to show us other characters doing something else at that same moment, the unifying factor ceases to be the individual personality but the moment of time which joins these diverse figures. And that moment is emphasized

64

throughout the book by the striking of a clock, denoting the exact hour. Whenever a clock strikes in *Mrs. Dalloway* it is because the author is going to move from one character to others, and is emphasizing the moment of time in virtue of which these disparate individuals are related. Characters are related to each other by existing contemporaneously, by coexistence in time: moments of time are related to each other by coexistence within the retrospecting mind of the individual.

There is in *Mrs. Dalloway* a regular alternation of these two methods: we are either moving freely in time within the consciousness of an individual, or moving from person to person at a single moment in time. Locality is emphasized at intervals in each monologue—"She had reached the Park gates"; "thought Mrs. Dalloway, coming out of Mulberry's"—and time is emphasized in moments of transition from one character to another. For example, at the opening of the book we are introduced first to Mrs. Dalloway, and immediately we are taken back, through her thought stream, into the past:

Mrs. Dalloway said she would buy the flowers herself.

For Lucy had her work cut out for her. The doors would be taken off their hinges; Rumpelmayer's men were coming. And then, thought Clarissa Dalloway, what a morning—fresh as if issued to children on a beach.

What a lark! What a plunge! For so it had always seemed to her, when, with a little squeak of the hinges, which she could hear now, she had burst open the French windows and plunged at Bourton into the open air. How fresh, how calm, stiller than this of course, the air was in the early morning; like the flap of a wave; the kiss of a wave; chill and sharp and yet (for a girl of eighteen as she then was) solemn, feeling as she did, standing

there at the open window, that something awful was about to
happen; looking at the flowers, at the trees with the smoke winding off them and the rooks rising, falling; standing and looking
until Peter Walsh said, "Musing among the vegetables?"—was
that it?—"I prefer men to cauliflowers"—was that it?

Virginia Woolf helps out the reader. The phrase "for
a girl of eighteen, as she then was," makes it plain that we
are here dealing with one of Mrs. Dalloway's recollections
of her youth. Virginia Woolf is always more courteous to
the reader than Joyce in this respect, for it is important
to her to give these signposts, indications of place (or of
the person who is doing the thinking) when time is fluid,
and indications of time when space is fluid (i.e., when she
is moving from person to person).

After a fairly lengthy account of Mrs. Dalloway's
thought stream—where we are now taken back into the
past, now brought forward into the present moment, when
Mrs. Dalloway is walking in a London street, and now seeing her thoughts turn to her party, which is to take place
that night—we are reminded, by the striking of Big Ben,
of the exact moment of time, and this prepares the way
for an account of other figures who at this same instant
are walking in London streets on errands of their own.
After hovering over a group of several figures, Virginia
Woolf eventually alights on one of them and we enter
his thought stream, to remain there until, with another
indication of the time of day, she again takes us to other
characters.[1]

[1] This point is elaborated, with diagrams, in the present writer's
book, *The Novel and the Modern World* (Univ. of Chicago Press,
1939), pp. 173–180.

THE SEMI-TRANSPARENT ENVELOPE

An interesting device for tying together the diverse groups of people to whom we are introduced in the first part of the book is the car with drawn blinds which, because it contains some royal personage or public dignitary, attracts the attention of all the persons in the neighbourhood who observe its progress. We first hear of it when a sudden blow-out startles Miss Pym, the florist, as she is helping Mrs. Dalloway to choose flowers:

"Dear, those motor cars," said Miss Pym, going to the window to look, and coming back and smiling apologetically with her hands full of sweet peas, as if those motor cars, those tyres of motor cars, were all *her* fault.

Then we get it used as a link between different characters:

The violent explosion which made Mrs. Dalloway jump and Miss Pym go to the window and apologise came from a motor car which had drawn to the side of the pavement precisely opposite Mulberry's shop window. Passers-by who, of course, stopped and stared, had just time to see a face of the very greatest importance against the dove-grey upholstery, before a male hand drew the blind and there was nothing to be seen except a square of dove grey.

Yet rumours were at once in circulation from the middle of Bond Street to Oxford Street on one side, to Atkinson's scent shop on the other, passing invisibly, inaudibly, like a cloud, swift, veil-like upon the hills, falling indeed with something of a cloud's sudden sobriety and stillness upon faces which a second before had been utterly disorderly. But now mystery had brushed them with her wing; they had heard the voice of authority; the spirit of religion was abroad with her eyes bandaged tight and her lips gaping wide. But nobody knew whose face had been seen. Was it the Prince of Wales's, the Queen's, the Prime Minister's? Whose face was it? Nobody knew.

Edgar J. Watkiss, with his roll of lead piping round his arm,

said audibly, humorously of course: "The Proime Minister's kyar."
Septimus Warren Smith, who found himself unable to pass,
heard him.

And at Septimus Warren Smith we pause. Soon the
reader finds himself alone with Smith and his wife, introduced to their thoughts, their problems, their plans.
(Smith is one of the principal characters in the book, Mrs.
Dalloway's anti-type, and at the same time her double.
An ex-soldier suffering from the delayed effects of shell-
shock, he is introduced to us at intervals throughout the
story as Mrs. Dalloway or other characters come into
casual contact with him, and his story is built up bit by
bit, partly through his own stream of consciousness, partly
by the author's objective description. Later on that afternoon he commits suicide when they come to take him
away to an asylum, and Sir William Bradshaw, the pomp-
ous specialist whose mishandling of the case has resulted
in this climax, comes to Mrs. Dalloway's party that evening
and casually mentions the young man's fate to her. This
results in a moment of luminous insight for Mrs. Dalloway in which, speculating on life and death and time, she
has a fleeting sense of indentity with the suicide. This
identification of Mrs. Dalloway with a young man whom
she has never known and whom she hears of for the first
time only after he is dead represents the final bringing
together of the threads in the story.)
The use of the car to relate certain characters with
each other is paralleled by similar devices throughout the
book. The aeroplane, for example, which is sky writing
in a clear sky, attracts the simultaneous attention of all
sorts of people in all parts of London, and enables Vir-

ginia Woolf to move from one to the other, using the aeroplane as a means of easy transition:

Suddenly Mrs. Coates looked up into the sky. The sound of an aeroplane bored ominously into the ears of the crowd. There it was coming over the trees, letting out white smoke from behind, which curled and twisted, actually writing something! making letters in the sky! Every one looked up . . .

"Glaxo," said Mrs. Coates in a strained, awe-stricken voice, gazing straight up, and her baby, lying stiff and white in her arms, gazed straight up.

"Kreemo," murmured Mrs. Bletchley, like a sleepwalker. With his hat held out perfectly still in his hand, Mr. Bowley gazed straight up. All down the Mall people were standing and looking up into the sky. As they looked the whole world became perfectly silent, and a flight of gulls crossed the sky, first one gull leading, then another, and in this extraordinary silence and peace, in this pallor, in this purity, bells struck eleven times, the sound fading up there among the gulls.

The aeroplane turned and raced and swooped exactly where it liked, swiftly, freely, like a skater—

"That's an E," said Mrs. Bletchley—
or a dancer—

"It's toffee," murmured Mr. Bowley—
(and the car went in at the gates and nobody looked at it), and shutting off the smoke, away and away it rushed, and the smoke faded and assembled itself round the broad white shapes of the clouds. . . .

Lucrezia Warren Smith, sitting by her husband's side on a seat in Regent's Park in the Broad Walk, looked up.

"Look, look, Septimus!" she cried. For Dr. Holmes had told her to make her husband (who had nothing whatever seriously the matter with him but was a little out of sorts) take an interest in things outside himself.

One notices here, too, the introduction of the striking clock—"bells struck eleven times"—to emphasize the single point of time as another unifying factor when the author has a number of diverse people on the scene simultaneously.

Virginia Woolf never attempts to transcribe the stream of consciousness of her characters directly, as Joyce does. It is always reported, with phrases such as "she thought" introduced regularly. She wants to keep control of the story as it progresses, to retain not only her directive power over the material but her ability to emphasize the unifying factor, which is, as we have seen, either the personality of the thinker or the single moment of time at which diverse people do diverse things. She therefore keeps reminding the reader whose stream of consciousness it is that he is reading, for this reminder is the unifying factor, just as the striking clocks are the unifying factor when she leaves an individual mind and goes from person to person.

The desire to transcribe the naked consciousness on to the printed page, so characteristic of a great deal of modern fiction, is in Virginia Woolf subordinated to the desire for intelligibility, form and organization. Joyce, it is true, who came much closer to the bare transcription of mental processes than Virginia Woolf ever did, was equally conscious of the need for pattern and organization, but he imposed his organization from without, by external devices (parallels with the *Odyssey;* each section corresponding to a different organ of the human body, a different art, a different colour, etc.) while Virginia Woolf, who wanted to make her novels corroborate a certain personal view of life, edited the thought process as she wrote it, giving it internal organization and pattern, selecting,

70

commenting, re-phrasing. While Joyce takes the raw material of consciousness and expands it into a summary of all existence by analogies with art, science and history, Virginia Woolf, avoiding all such elaborate analogies, makes her points by the way she selects and organizes her reports of thought processes. Joyce analogizes to compensate for lack of selection, but Virginia Woolf, who selects and refines as she writes, has no need of such a device. For her novels are intended to present a personal point of view about life, while Joyce's problem is to present all points of view simultaneously.

Virginia Woolf had a tidy mind, and she was not content to allow the thought stream of her characters to meander on without apparent purpose. She was even anxious to indicate to the reader a certain necessary, logical connection between one part of a reverie and the next. She was aware that the "free association" which makes up so much of our mental processes did not proceed in any logical order, yet it was logical in a sense, there was some deep and unconscious logic connecting these apparently random thoughts and images that crowd the drifting mind. Virginia Woolf indicates this pseudo-logic by introducing almost every new turn in a reverie with the word "for"—a word which does not indicate a strict logical sequence, at least not in its popular usage, but does suggest a relationship which is at least half-logical. Here, for example, is Mrs. Dalloway recalling the past and at the same time taking note of the present:

She could remember scene after scene at Bourton—Peter furious; Hugh not, of course, his match in any way, but still not a positive imbecile as Peter made out; not a mere barber's block. When his old mother wanted him to give up shooting or to take her to Bath he did it, without a word; he was really unselfish, and as for saying, as Peter did, that he had no heart, no brain, nothing but the manners and breeding of an English gentleman, that was only her dear Peter at his worst; and he could be intolerable; he could be impossible; but adorable to walk with on a morning like this.

(June had drawn out every leaf on the trees. The mothers of Pimlico gave suck to their young. Messages were passing from the Fleet to the Admiralty. Arlington Street and Piccadilly seemed to chafe the very air in the Park and lift its leaves hotly, brilliantly, on waves of that divine vitality which Clarissa loved. To dance, to ride, she had adored all that.)

For they might be parted for hundreds of years, she and Peter; she never wrote a letter and his were dry sticks; but suddenly it would come over her, If he were with me now what would he say?

The "for" which introduces the last paragraph here has a very precise function. It indicates the inexplicable half-logic of reverie.

It is interesting to note how Virginia Woolf maintains her compromise between reported thought and direct, unedited transcription of consciousness. That transitional pronoun "one," midway between the first and the third person in its implications, is called on to help out, and we can often see the ebb and flow between the subjective and the objective attitudes:

For having lived in Westminster—how many years now? over twenty,—one feels even in the midst of the traffic, or waking at night, Clarissa was positive, a particular hush, or solemnity; an indescribable pause; a suspense (but that might be her heart, affected, they said, by influenza) before Big Ben strikes. There! Out it boomed. First a warning, musical; then the hour, irrevocable. The leaden circles dissolved in the air. Such fools we are, she thought, crossing Victoria Street. For Heaven only knows why one loves it so, how one sees it so. . . .

In the first phrase the first personal pronoun is implied, and we move from this through the indeterminate "one feels" to the third person, "Clarissa was positive." We notice, also, in this passage, the characteristic use of the present participle to allow the author to remind the reader of the character's position without interrupting the thought stream—"she thought, crossing Victoria Street." This is a very common device.

The pronoun "one" serves another function. It indicates a certain agreement on the part of the author with the character's thoughts. Whenever the character is embarked on a speculation which is directly relevant to the main theme of the book (i.e., with which Virginia Woolf herself would agree) the pronoun tends to be indefinite. "Clarissa thought" would introduce the particular thought of a particular character, but to introduce the speculation "one imagines" suggests that it is a more universal experience, and one which the author shares. Thus this very minor device helps Virginia Woolf to make her novels presentations of her own view of life.

And *Mrs. Dalloway* is the presentation of a view of life. There is a suggestion throughout that the experiences of individuals combine to form a single indeterminate whole, and that wisdom is the recognition of this. Her characters are shown as reaching their moments of greatest insight when they perceive life as that "luminous halo" which Virginia Woolf had already in her own person declared it to be. This is the view that underlies *Jacob's Room* as it underlies *Mrs. Dalloway* and all the subsequent novels. It is this idea alone that makes sense of the reverie of Mrs. Dalloway after she has learned from Sir William

Bradshaw of the death of the unknown young man:

What business had the Bradshaws to talk of death at her party?
A young man had killed himself. And they talked of it at her
party—the Bradshaws talked of death. He had killed himself—
but how? Always her body went through it first, when she was
told, suddenly, of an accident; her dress flamed, her body burnt.
He had thrown himself from a window. Up had flashed the ground;
through him, blundering, bruising, went the rusty spikes. There
he lay with a thud, thud, thud in his brain, and then a suffocation
of blackness. So she saw it. But why had he done it? And the
Bradshaws talked of it at her party!

She had once thrown a shilling into the Serpentine, never anything more. But he had flung it away. They went on living (she
would have to go back; the rooms were still crowded; people kept
on coming). They (all day she had been thinking of Bourton, of
Peter, of Sally), they would grow old. A thing there was that mat-
tered; a thing, wreathed about with chatter, defaced, obscured in
her own life, let drop every day in corruption, lies, chatter. This
he had preserved. Death was defiance. Death was an attempt to
communicate; people feeling the impossibility of reaching the
centre which, mystically, evaded them; closeness drew apart; rapture faded, one was alone. There was an embrace in death.

But this young man who had killed himself—had he plunged
holding his treasure? "If it were now to die, 'twere now to be
most happy," she had said to herself once, coming down in white.

And again:

She parted the curtains; she looked. Oh, but how surprising!—
in the room opposite the old lady stared straight at her! She was
going to bed. And the sky. It will be a solemn sky, she had thought,
it will be a dusky sky, turning away its cheek in beauty. But there
it was—ashen pale, raced over by tapering vast clouds. It was
new to her. The wind must have risen. She was going to bed, in
the room opposite. It was fascinating to watch her, moving about,
that old lady, crossing the room, coming to the window. Could
she see her? It was fascinating, with people still laughing and

shouting in the drawing-room, to watch that old woman, quite quietly, going to bed. She pulled the blind now. The clock began striking. The young man had killed himself; but she did not pity him; with the clock striking the hour, one, two, three, she did not pity him, with all this going on. There! the old lady had put out her light! the whole house was dark now with this going on, she repeated, and the words came to her, Fear no more the heat of the sun. She must go back to them. But what an extraordinary night! She felt somehow very like him—the young man who had killed himself. She felt glad that he had done it; thrown it away. The clock was striking. The leaden circles dissolved in the air. He made her feel the beauty; made her feel the fun. But she must go back. She must assemble. She must find Sally and Peter. And she came in from the little room.

The identification of Mrs. Dalloway with Septimus Warren Smith is not an arbitrary piece of plot resolution; it arises from the underlying view of experience as a unified flux, in which even the most disparate individuals can make contact with each other. Virginia Woolf tells us, in a preface written three years after the book was first published, that "in the first version Septimus, who later is intended to be her double, had no existence; and that Mrs. Dalloway was originally to kill herself at the end of the party." Mrs. Dalloway, that is, was originally to lose herself in the flux of experience by dying, while later the same idea was more subtly expressed by making her identify herself with an unknown young man who had already died. This preoccupation with time, death and personality and their relations with each other we shall discuss again in dealing with Virginia Woolf's later works.

In *Mrs. Dalloway* Virginia Woolf achieved the sensitive organization of tenuous insights which she had earlier come to consider the function of the novelist. The organization of the work reminds one more of a lyric poem than anything else. A mood is expressed through the patterning of symbolic imagery:

Such are the visions. The solitary traveller is soon beyond the wood; and there, coming to the door with shaded eyes, possibly to look for his return, with hands raised, with white apron blowing, is an elderly woman who seems (so powerful is this infirmity) to seek, over a desert, a lost son; to search for a rider destroyed; to be the figure of the mother whose sons have been killed in the battles of the world. So, as the solitary traveller advances down the village street where the women stand knitting and the men dig in the garden, the evening seems ominous; the figures still; as if some august fate, known to them, awaited without fear, were about to sweep them into complete annihilation.

Indoors among ordinary things, the cupboard, the table, the window-sill with its geraniums, suddenly the outline of the landlady, bending to remove the cloth, becomes soft with light, an adorable emblem which only the recollection of cold human contacts forbids us to embrace. She takes the marmalade; she shuts it in the cupboard.

"There is nothing more to-night, sir?"

But to whom does the solitary traveller make reply?

The significant moments in experience are the moments of insight, which can be expressed only symbolically:

It was all over for her. The sheet was stretched and the bed narrow. She had gone up into the tower and left them blackberrying in the sun. The door had shut, and there among the dust of fallen plaster and the litter of birds' nests how distant the view had looked, and the sounds came thin and chill (once on Leith Hill, she remembered), and Richard, Richard! she cried, as a sleeper in the night starts and stretches a hand in the dark for help. Lunching with Lady Brouton, it came back to her. He has left me; I am alone for ever, she thought, folding her hands upon her knee.

76

THE SEMI-TRANSPARENT ENVELOPE

The question for the critic is whether the process of rarification which goes on throughout the novel does not end by denuding it of a certain necessary vitality. Here is London in the summer of 1919, with life humming and bustling around Mrs. Dalloway as she goes out to buy flowers for her party, and yet all this life emerges as fragmentary insights, snatches of suggestive imagery, tenuous meditation. Is there not, one asks, a certain over-refinement here, has not reality been whittled down to almost nothing? And why, if the aim is to present a subtle lyrical-cum-philosophical interpretation of experience, is the action set so solidly in upper middle-class urban life? Is the contrast between the bourgeois solidity of Mrs. Dalloway's environment and the nature of her own consciousness meant to be part of the effect? Sometimes the very sensibility seems rooted in middle-class leisure:

Beauty anyhow. Not the crude beauty of the eye. It was not beauty pure and simple—Bedford Place leading into Russell Square. It was straightness and emptiness of course; the symmetry of a corridor; but it was also windows lit up, a piano, a gramophone sounding; a sense of pleasure-making hidden, but now and again emerging when, through the uncurtained window, the window left open, one saw parties sitting over tables, young people slowly circling, conversations between men and women, maids idly looking out (a strange comment theirs, when work was done), stockings drying on top ledges, a parrot, a few plants. Absorbing, mysterious, of infinite richness, this life. And in the large square where the cabs shot and swerved so quick, there were loitering couples, dallying, embracing, shrunk up under the shower of a tree; that was moving; so silent, so absorbed, that one passed, discreetly, timidly, as if in the presence of some sacred ceremony to interrupt which would have been impious. That was interesting. And so on into the flare and glare.

Every now and again in Virginia Woolf's work we sense the unconscious implication that sensibility is the prerogative of the more leisured and intelligent members of the middle class. Not that she is complacent in her acceptance of middle-class standards: far from it: perhaps the majority of her middle-class characters are portrayed satirically, while her picture of the aristocracy in *Mrs. Dalloway* shows no illusions. But there are passages in her work that are more reminiscent of Galsworthy's "Indian Summer of a Forsyte" than she would ever have admitted.

The dissolution of experience into tenuous insights— this is the real theme of the most important part of Virginia Woolf's work, and it is the real theme of *Mrs. Dalloway*. The lack of background, the lack of moral base or generally accepted standards, which distinguish a work of this kind so sharply from any of the great novels of the nineteenth century, give it at the same time qualities of its own. There is a sophistication of sensibility here, a personal delicacy in the treatment of moods and emotions, which give the book a certain lyrical power which the experienced reader is wholly unable to resist. It is, perhaps, an Alexandrian art, but there can be no doubt that, within its limits, it is both accomplished and effective. And if we have the feeling that the raw material of life was carefully refined in the study before the author proceeded to deal with it in fiction, that is a feeling appropriate to a work of this kind, personal, insubstantial, sophisticated. At the very least, one can say that this sort of work could never have been produced without intelligence. Indeed, intelligence here seems to create its own sensibility as it moves.

THE SEMI-TRANSPARENT ENVELOPE

Two years after *Mrs. Dalloway* there appeared the book which marks the perfection of Virginia Woolf's art: *To the Lighthouse*. Here, instead of taking a group of characters in upper middle-class London society and wringing some rarified meaning out of their states of mind, she keeps her characters throughout the novel on an island in the Hebrides, an island unparticularized and remote, which, by its setting and associations, helps her to break down the apparent concreteness of character and events into that "luminous halo" which for her was the most adequate symbol of life. The basic plot framework is simple enough. The book is divided into three sections: the first "The Window," deals with Mr. and Mrs. Ramsay, their children and their guests on holiday on the island one late September day a few years before the first World War; the second, "Time Passes," gives an impressionist rendering of the change and decay which their house on the island suffers in the years following: the war prevents the family from revisiting the place, Mrs. Ramsay dies, Andrew Ramsay is killed in the war, Prue Ramsay dies in childbirth—all this is suggested parenthetically in the course of the account of the decay of the house; in the third and final section, "The Lighthouse," we see the remnant of the Ramsay family revisiting their house on the island some ten years later, with some of the same guests, and the book closes with Lily Briscoe, a guest on both visits, completing a picture she had begun on the first visit—completing it in the light of the vision which finally comes to her and enables her to see for a moment in their proper relation the true significance of the dead Mrs. Ramsay, of the whole Ramsay family, and of the physical scene in

79

front of her. A further tie-up is effected in the actual visit to the lighthouse made by Mr. Ramsay and two of the children in the last section: this visit had been planned in the first section, but had been put off owing to bad weather, much to the disappointment of young James Ramsay and his mother, and so the visit, when it actually takes place years after Mrs. Ramsay's death, with James no longer a small boy but an adolescent, has a certain symbolic meaning. The arrival of the Ramsays at the lighthouse, and Lily Briscoe's achievement of her vision as she sits in front of the Ramsay's house painting and meditating, occur contemporaneously, and this conjunction possesses further symbolic significance.

Upon this framework Virginia Woolf weaves a delicate pattern of symbolic thoughts and situations. The book opens with a certain deliberate abruptness:

"Yes, of course, if it's fine tomorrow," said Mrs. Ramsay. "But you'll have to be up with the lark," she added.

She is referring to the expedition to the lighthouse, on which young James, aged six, had set his heart. The planning and eventual accomplishment of this expedition constitute the main principle of integration employed by Virginia Woolf to unify the story. Following the opening remark of Mrs. Ramsay come James's reactions:

To her son these words conveyed an extraordinary joy, as if it were settled, the expedition were bound to take place, and the wonder to which he had looked forward, for years and years it seemed, was, after a night's darkness and a day's sail, within touch. Since he belonged, even at the age of six, to that great clan which cannot keep this feeling separate from that, but must let future prospects, with their joys and sorrows, cloud what is actually at hand, since to such people even in earliest childhood any turn in the wheel of sensation has the power to crystallise and transfix the moment upon which its gloom or radiance rests, James Ramsay, sitting on the floor cutting out pictures from the illustrated catalogue of the Army and Navy Stores, endowed the picture of a refrigerator, as his mother spoke, with heavenly bliss. It was fringed with joy. The wheelbarrow, the lawnmower, the sound of poplar trees, leaves whitening before rain, rooks cawing, brooms knocking, dresses rustling—all these were so coloured and distinguished in his mind that he had already his private code, his secret language, though he appeared the image of stark and uncompromising severity, with his high forehead and his fierce blue eyes, impeccably candid and pure, frowning slightly at the sight of human frailty, so that his mother, watching him guide his scissors neatly round the refriger ator, imagined him all red and ermine on the Bench or directing a stern and momentous enterprise in some crisis of public affairs.

Here is a careful weaving together of character's consciousness, author's comment, and one character's view of another. On James's happy expectation crashes his father's ruthless remarks:

"But," said his father, stopping in front of the drawing-room window, "it won't be fine."

This remark arouses in James a fierce, frustrated anger. "Had there been an axe handy, or a poker, any weapon that would have gashed a hole in his father's breast and killed him, there and then, James would have seized it." Mr. Ramsay was always right, and James knew that his prophecy could not be laughed off. But his anger at his father's deliberate dashing of his hopes was increased rather than modified by this knowledge, and the grudge entered into his subconscious to be finally exorcized only when, ten years later, they arrive at the lighthouse and

Mr. Ramsay turns and compliments James on his steering of the boat.

Virginia Woolf's handling of this point is, however, much subtler than this bald summary would suggest. For the theme is symbolic in its implications, and in her elaboration of it Virginia Woolf not only brings out the full character of James and his father, establishes their complex relation to each other, indicates the relation of Mr. Ramsay to the other characters and their relation to him, and illuminates some general problems concerning the relation of parents to children, husband to wife, and people to each other, but also endeavours to suggest indirectly certain profound ideas about experience and its dependence on time and personality. What is the most significant quality in experience? This is the question which *To the Lighthouse* seems designed to answer. In what sense can one personality ever "know" another? What relation do our various memories of a single object bear to the "real" object? What remains when a personality has been "spilt on air" and exists only as a group of contradictory impressions in others, who are also moving towards death? In what way does time condition human experience and its values? Out of that complex of retrospect and anticipation which is consciousness, what knowledge can emerge, what vision can be achieved? These are further problems which the book's form and content are designed to illuminate.

And so, with this limited collection of characters—the Ramsays and their guests—Virginia Woolf passes from one consciousness to another, from one group to another, exploring the significance of their reactions, following the course of their meditations, carefully arranging and patterning the images that rise up in their minds, bringing together, with care and economy, a select number of symbolic incidents, until a design has been achieved, the solidity of objective things breaks down, and experience is seen as something fluid though with definite shape, inexpressible yet significant.

In *Mrs. Dalloway* Virginia Woolf set the scene of her action with precision. We know at any given moment what part of London we are in. Streets and buildings are given their real names, and carefully particularized. But in *To the Lighthouse* for the first time in a full-length novel Virginia Woolf reduces the particularizing details of the setting to a minimum. We know, from one fleeting reference, that we are on an island in the Hebrides [1] but

[1] There are precisely three indications of the locality of the setting in *To the Lighthouse*. "Scotland" is mentioned on page 44 (Harcourt, Brace Edition): "and no lockmaker in the whole of Scotland can mend a bolt." A map of the Hebrides is referred to on page 170. And when Minta loses her brooch, Paul resolves that if he could not find it "he would slip out of the house at dawn when they were all asleep and if he could not find it he would go to Edinburgh and buy her another." Glasgow, however, and not Edinburgh would be the obvious city to go to if they were anywhere in the Hebrides, so this reference is misleading. The present writer, who knows the west coast of Scotland, has amused himself by trying to pin down the island, but has found that it is impossible to do so. The details given by Virginia Woolf are at once too general to be identified with any particular place and too specific (position of the beach, distance from the lighthouse, relation to "the town," type of vegetation, etc.) to be made to fit in with any spot chosen at random. What island in the Hebrides is there, large enough to contain a "town" (p. 18, etc.), yet small enough to appear "very small," "like a thin leaf," when one had sailed only a few miles away; possessing both cliffs, "park-like prospects," trees, sandy beach, sand dunes (p. 105), accommo-

that is all the information we get. For the rest, we learn that the Ramsay's house is within walking distance of the "town" and situated on a bay. It is clear that Virginia Woolf is here more concerned with conveying a general impression of sea, sand and rocks than with describing any particular place. It is a symbolic setting: this group of people temporarily isolated from the rest of society on this remote island represents a microcosm of society, while the background of natural scenery provides images and suggestions that can be used as interpretative symbols. Throughout the book the characters are presented and re-presented until they are finally seen as symbolic. We are shown now their own minds, now their reactions on the minds of others, now the memory they leave when they are gone, now their relation to the landscape, till eventually all this adds up to something barely expressible (indeed not directly expressible at all) yet significant. For a split second everything falls into a pattern, and then the meaning is lost again, as (to employ a simile that keeps recurring in *To the Lighthouse*) we look out of the windows of a speeding train and see for one brief moment a group of figures that conveys some strange new meaning. With the temporary attainment of maximum pattern the book ends. Lily Briscoe, the painter, the spinster who will not marry and keeps looking for the proper significance of characters and scenes, is deputy for the author:

---

dating at walking distance from the "town" a large house with lawn, cultivated garden, tennis court, and other amenities, and with local inhabitants named McNab (the charwoman) and Macalister (the boatman). Neither Macallister nor McNab is an Island name. Virginia Woolf's scene is either a composite one (with perhaps some suggestions from Cornwall) or largely imaginary.

when she, thinking of the now dead Mrs. Ramsay and of Mr. Ramsay off in the boat to the lighthouse, and endeavouring at the same time to find the proper way of finishing her picture, finally has her "vision," the pattern is complete, she finishes her painting, and the book ends. The Ramsays have at last landed at the lighthouse. Lily Briscoe, thinking of them as she paints, recognizes their landing as somehow significant. So does old Mr. Carmichael, who has been dozing in a chair on the lawn not far from her. And the final threads come together:

"He has landed," she said aloud. "It is finished." Then, surging up, puffing slightly, old Mr. Carmichael stood beside her, looking like an old pagan god, shaggy, with weeds in his hair and the trident (it was only a French novel) in his hand. He stood by her on the edge of the lawn, swaying a little in his bulk, and said, shading his eyes with his hand: "They will have landed," and she felt that she had been right. They had not needed to speak. They had been thinking the same things and he had answered her without her asking him anything. He stood there as if he were spreading his hands over all the weakness and suffering of mankind; she thought he was surveying, tolerantly and compassionately, their final destiny. Now he has crowned the occasion, she thought, when his hand slowly fell, as if she had seen him let fall from his great height a wreath of violets and asphodels which, fluttering slowly, lay at length upon the earth.

Quickly, as if she were recalled by something over there, she turned to her canvas. There it was—her picture. Yes, with all its greens and blues, its lines running up and across, its attempt at something. It would be hung in the attics, she thought; it would be destroyed. But what did that matter? she asked herself, taking up her brush again. She looked at the steps; they were empty; she looked at her canvas; it was blurred. With a sudden intensity, as if she saw it clear for a second, she drew a line there, in the centre. It was done; it was finished. Yes, she thought, laying down her brush in extreme fatigue, I have had my vision.

The characters in *To the Lighthouse* are carefully arranged in their relation to each other, so that a definite symbolic pattern emerges. Mr. Ramsay, the professor of philosophy, who made one original contribution to thought in his youth and has since been repeating and elaborating it without being able to see through to the ultimate implications of his system; his wife, who knows more of life in an unsystematic and intuitive way, who has no illusions ("There was no treachery too base for the world to commit; she knew that. No happiness lasted; she knew that.") yet presides over her family with a calm and competent efficiency; Lily Briscoe, who refuses to get married and tries to express her sense of reality in terms of colour and form; Charles Tansley, the aggressive young philosopher with an inferiority complex; old Mr. Carmichael, who dozes unsocially in the sun and eventually turns out to be a lyric poet; Minta Doyle and Paul Rayley, the undistinguished couple whom Mrs. Ramsay gently urges into a not too successful marriage—each character has a very precise function in this carefully organized story. The lighthouse itself, standing lonely in the midst of the sea, is a symbol of the individual who is at once a unique being and a part of the flux of history. To reach the lighthouse is, in a sense, to make contact with a truth outside oneself, to surrender the uniqueness of one's ego to an impersonal reality. Mr. Ramsay, who is an egotist constantly seeking applause and encouragement from others, resents his young son's enthusiasm for visiting the lighthouse, and only years later, when his wife has died and his own life is almost worn out, does he win this freedom from self—and it is significant that Virginia Woolf makes Mr. Ramsay escape from his egotistic preoccupations for the first time just before the boat finally reaches the lighthouse. Indeed, the personal grudges nourished by each of the characters fall away just as they arrive; Mr. Ramsay ceases to pose with his book and breaks out with an exclamation of admiration for James's steering; James and his sister Cam lose their resentment at their father's way of bullying them into this expedition and cease hugging their grievances: "What do you want? they both wanted to ask. They both wanted to say, Ask us anything and we will give it you. But he did not ask them anything." And at the moment when they land, Lily Briscoe and old Mr. Carmichael, who had not joined the expedition, suddenly develop a mood of tolerance and compassion for mankind, and Lily has the vision which enables her to complete her picture.

There is a colour symbolism running right through the book. When Lily Briscoe is wrestling unsuccessfully with her painting, in the first part of the book, she sees the colours as "bright violet and staring white," but just as she achieves her final vision at the book's conclusion, and is thus able to complete her picture, she notices that the lighthouse "had melted away into a blue haze"; and though she sees the canvas clearly for a second before drawing the final line, the implication remains that this blurring of colours is bound up with her vision. Mr. Ramsay, who visualizes the last, unattainable, step in his philosophy as glimmering *red* in the distance, is contrasted with the less egotistical Lily, who works with blues and greens, and with Mrs. Ramsay, who is indicated on Lily's canvas as "a triangular purple shape." Red and brown appear to be the colours of individuality and egotism, while blue and green are the colours of impersonality. Mr. Ramsay, until the very end of the book, is represented as an egotist, and his colour is red or brown; Lily is the impersonal artist, and her colour is blue; Mrs. Ramsay stands somewhere between, and her colour is purple.[1] The journey to the lighthouse is the journey from egotism to impersonality.

But it is much more than that. The story opens with Mrs. Ramsay promising young James that if it is fine they will go to the lighthouse tomorrow, whereupon Mr. Ram-

[1] There is a beautiful example of this colour symbolism on p. 270 (Harcourt, Brace Edition): "Wherever she happened to be, painting, here, in the country or in London, the vision would come to her, and her eyes, half closing, sought something to base her vision on. She looked down the railway carriage, the omnibus; took a line from shoulder or cheek; looked at the windows opposite; at Piccadilly, lamp-strung in the evening. All had been part of the fields of death. But always something—it might be a face, a voice, a paper boy crying *Standard*, *News*—thrust through, snubbed her, waked her, required and got in the end an effort of attention, so that the vision must be perpetually remade. Now again, moved as she was by some instinctive need of distance and blue, she looked at the bay beneath her, making hillocks of the blue bars of the waves, and stony fields of the purpler spaces, again she was roused as usual by something incongruous. There was a brown spot in the middle of the bay. It was a boat. Yes, she realised that after a second. But whose boat? Mr. Ramsay's boat, she replied. Mr. Ramsay; the man who had marched past her, with his hand raised, aloof, at the head of a procession, in his beautiful boots, asking her for sympathy, which she had refused. The boat was now half way across the bay."

This passage, while taking its place naturally in the development of the story, at the same time throws an important light on the earlier and later parts of the book, clarifying symbolism and enriching significance. The artist, having an "instinctive need of . . . blue," sees Mr. Ramsay's boat as a *brown* spot on a *blue* sea. Brown is the personal colour, the egotistic colour; blue belongs to the impersonality of the artist.

say points out that it won't be fine, and arouses James's long lived resentment. It concludes, ten years later when Mrs. Ramsay is dead and James is sixteen, with the arrival of Mr. Ramsay, James and Cam at the lighthouse and the shedding at that moment of all their personal grudges and resentments—all of which synchronize with Lily's achievement of her vision. The story is obviously more than the contrast between the initial and the final situation, for between these two points there is an abundance of detail—description of character and of characters' thought processes—and a number of symbolic situations which widen the implications of the book as it proceeds and prevents the reader from identifying its meaning with any single "moral."

The theme of the relation of the individual to existence as a whole is treated in a variety of ways. It recurs as a constantly shifting thought pattern in character after character. Lily Briscoe, the artist, is observing Mr. Ramsay, philosopher and egotist:

Lily Briscoe went on putting away her brushes, looking up, looking down. Looking up, there he was—Mr. Ramsay—advancing towards them, swinging, careless, oblivious, remote. A bit of a hypocrite? she repeated. Oh, no—the most sincere of men, the truest (here he was), the best; but, looking down, she thought, he is absorbed in himself, he is tyrannical, he is unjust; and kept looking down, purposely, for only so could she keep steady, staying with the Ramsays. Directly one looked up and saw them, what she called "being in love" flooded them. They became part of that unreal but penetrating and exciting universe which is the world seen through the eyes of love. The sky stuck to them; the birds sang through them. And, what was even more exciting, she felt, too, as she saw Mr. Ramsay bearing down and retreating, and Mrs. Ramsay sitting with James in the window and the cloud

89

moving and the tree bending, how life, from being made up of
little separate incidents which one lived one by one, became curled
and whole like a wave which bore one up with it and threw one
down with it, there, with a dash on the beach.

Speculations of this kind are constantly juxtaposed to
specific incidents, which take on a symbolic quality in the
light of the juxtaposition:

Standing now, apparently transfixed, by the pear tree, impressions poured in upon her of those two men, and to follow
her thought was like following a voice which speaks too quickly
to be taken down by one's pencil, and the voice was her own
voice saying without prompting undeniable, everlasting, contradictory things, so that even the fissures and humps on the bark
of the pear tree were irrevocably fixed there for eternity. You have
greatness, she continued, but Mr. Ramsay has none of it. He is
petty, selfish, vain, egotistical; he is spoilt; he is a tyrant; he
wears Mrs. Ramsay to death; but he has what you (she addressed
Mr. Bankes) have not; a fiery unworldliness; he knows nothing
about trifles; he loves dogs and his children. He has eight. Mr.
Bankes has none. Did he not come down in two coats the other
night and let Mrs. Ramsay trim his hair into a pudding basin? All
of this danced up and down, like a company of gnats, each separate, but all marvellously controlled in an invisible elastic net—
danced up and down in Lily's mind, in and about the branches
of the pear tree, where still hung in effigy the scrubbed kitchen
table, symbol of her profound respect for Mr. Ramsay's mind,
until her thought which had spun quicker and quicker exploded
of its own intensity; she felt released; a shot went off close at
hand, and there came, flying from its fragments, frightened, ef-
fusive, tumultuous, a flock of starlings.

"Jasper!" said Mr. Bankes. They turned the way the starlings
flew, over the terrace. Following the scatter of swift-flying birds
in the sky they stepped through the gap in the high hedge straight
into Mr. Ramsay, who boomed tragically at them, "Some one had
blundered!"

90

THE SEMI-TRANSPARENT ENVELOPE

The stream of consciousness of one character enables us to see individual actions of other characters in their proper symbolic meaning. It is a subtle and effective device.

It would take too much space to discuss the minor devices employed by Virginia Woolf in order to help expand the meaning into something profounder yet vaguer than any specific thesis. The main theme concerns the relation of personality, death, and time to each other; the relation of the individual to the sum of experience in general. Many devices are used to suggest this problem—presented less as a problem than as a situation, a quality in life on which the significance of living depends. Minor points such as the characteristic gesture of Mr. Ramsay (raising his hand as if to avert something), symbolic images such as the hand cleaving the blue sea, specific ideas suggested in the thought process of one or other of the characters (each of whom can be made at any time to speak for the author by any one of a number of devices which present that character as having momentarily transcended the limitations of his personality and glimpsed some kind of eternal truth)—all help to enrich the implications of the story. Here, for example, is Lily Briscoe, symbol of the artist and his relation to experience:

She wanted to go straight up to him and say, "Mr. Carmichael!" Then he would look up benevolently as always, from his smoky vague green eyes. But one only woke people if one knew what one wanted to say to them. And she wanted to say not one thing, but everything. Little words that broke up the thought and dismembered it said nothing. "About life, about death; about Mrs. Ramsay"—no, she thought, one could say nothing to nobody. The urgency of the moment always missed its mark. Words fluttered sideways and struck the object inches too low. Then one gave it up; then the idea sunk back again; then one became like most middle-aged people, cautious, furtive, with wrinkles between the eyes and a look of perpetual apprehension. For how could one express in words these emotions of the body? express that emptiness there? (She was looking at the drawing-room steps; they looked extraordinarily empty.) It was one's body feeling, not one's mind. The physical sensations that went with the bare look of the steps had become suddenly extremely unpleasant. . . . Oh, Mrs. Ramsay! she called out silently, to that essence which sat by the boat, that abstract one made of her, that woman in grey, as if to abuse her for having gone, and then having gone, come back again. It had seemed so safe, thinking of her. Ghost, air, nothingness, a thing you could play with easily and safely at any time of day or night, she had been that, and then suddenly she put her hand out and wrung the heart thus. . . .

"What does it mean? How do you explain it all?" she wanted to say, turning to Mr. Carmichael again. For the whole world seemed to have dissolved in this early morning hour into a pool of thought, a deep basin of reality, and one could almost fancy that had Mr. Carmichael spoken, for instance, a little tear would have rent the surface pool. And then? Something would emerge. A hand would be shoved up, a blade would be flashed. It was nonsense of course.

Here the thoughts and images contained in a character's reverie reflect back and forth on other aspects of the story and enrich the meaning of the whole.

Finally, the reader might ponder on the symbolism of the window in the first section. Mr. Ramsay paces up and down in the growing darkness outside, while Mrs. Ramsay and James sit by the window, watching him pass back and forth. There is a detailed symbolism here, as deliberate, though not so obvious, as that of Maeterlinck's *Interior*.

Virginia Woolf's characteristic concern with the relation of personality to time, change and death is manifested in her treatment of the character of Mrs. Ramsay, who is alive in the first section and whose death is recorded parenthetically in the "Time Passes" interlude. Yet her personality dominates the book: she lives, in section three, in the memory of the others; her character has become part of history, including and determining the present. As she is about to finish her painting Lily Briscoe thinks of Mrs. Ramsay as still influential after death:

Mrs. Ramsay, she thought, stepping back and screwing up her eyes. (It must have altered the design a good deal when she was sitting on the step with James. There must have been a shadow.) When she thought of herself and Charles throwing ducks and drakes and of the whole scene on the beach, it seemed to depend somehow upon Mrs. Ramsay sitting under the rock, with a pad on her knee, writing letters. (She wrote innumerable letters, and sometimes the wind took them and she and Charles just saved a page from the sea.) But what a power was in the human soul! she thought. That woman sitting there writing under the rock resolved everything into simplicity; made these angers, irritations fall off like old rags; she brought together this and that and then this, and so made out of that miserable silliness and spite (she and Charles squabbling, sparring, had been silly and spiteful) something—this scene on the beach for example, this moment of friendship and liking—which survived, after all these years complete, so that she dipped into it to re-fashion her memory of him, and there it stayed in the mind affecting one almost like a work of art.

And she goes on to speculate on the present significance of the woman who had been dead now for five years:

What is the meaning of life? That was all—a simple question; one that tended to close in on one with years. The great revelation had never come. The great revelation perhaps never did come. Instead there were little daily miracles, illuminations, matches struck unexpectedly in the dark; here was one. This, that, and the other; herself and Charles Tansley and the breaking wave; Mrs. Ramsay bringing them together; Mrs. Ramsay saying, "Life stand still here"; Mrs. Ramsay making of the moment something permanent (as in another sphere Lily herself tried to make of the moment something permanent)—this was of the nature of a revelation. In the midst of chaos there was shape; this eternal passing and flowing (she looked at the clouds going and the leaves shaking) was struck into stability. Life stand still here, Mrs. Ramsay said. "Mrs. Ramsay! Mrs. Ramsay!" she repeated. She owed it all to her.

One can compare this with the reverie of Mrs. Dalloway on learning of the death of Septimus Warren Smith; the way of relating one character to another is not dissimilar. And just as, at the end of the former book, Mrs. Dalloway suddenly has her final illumination after she has watched the old woman opposite go into her bedroom and pull down the blind, so Lily, sitting painting outside the Ramsay's house, sees, just before her final vision, somebody come into the room behind the window:

Suddenly the window at which she was looking was whitened by some light stuff behind it. At last then somebody had come into the drawing-room; somebody was sitting in the chair. For Heaven's sake, she prayed, let them sit still there and not come floundering out to talk to her. Mercifully, whoever it was stayed still inside; had settled by some stroke of luck so as to throw an odd-shaped triangular shadow over the step. It altered the composition of the picture a little. It was interesting. It might be useful. Her mood was coming back to her. One must keep on looking without for a second relaxing the intensity of emotion, the determination not to be put off, not to be bamboozled. One must hold the scene—so—in a vise and let nothing come in and spoil it. One wanted, she thought, dipping her brush deliberately, to be on a level with ordinary experience, to feel simply that's a chair, that's a table, and yet at the same time, It's a miracle, it's an ecstasy. The problem might be solved after all. Ah, but what had happened? Some wave of white went over the window pane. The air must have stirred some flounce in the room. Her heart leapt at her and seized her and tortured her.

"Mrs. Ramsay! Mrs. Ramsay!" she cried, feeling the old horror come back—to want and want and not to have. Could she inflict that still? And then, quietly, as if she refrained, that too became part of ordinary experience, was on a level with the chair, with the table. Mrs. Ramsay—it was part of her perfect goodness— sat there quite simply, in the chair, flicked her needles to and fro, knitted her reddish-brown stocking, cast her shadow on the step. There she sat.

Symbolically, the past returns and shapes the present. Mrs. Ramsay comes back into Lily Briscoe's picture, as she had been part of the original design ten years before, and out of this meeting of two very different personalities across the years the final insight results. Across the water at the same moment Mr. Ramsay, by his praise of James's handling of the boat, is exorcising the ghost of James's early resentment, also ten years old, and all the threads of the story are finally coming together. It is a masterly piece of construction.

To the Lighthouse is a work in which plot, locale, and treatment are so carefully bound up with each other that the resulting whole is more finely organized and more effective than anything else Virginia Woolf wrote. The setting in an indefinite island off the north-west coast of Scotland enables her to indulge in her characteristic symbolic rarifications with maximum effect, for here form and content fit perfectly and inevitably. Middle-class London is not, perhaps, the best scene for a tenuous meditative work of this kind, and *Mrs. Dalloway* might be said to suffer from a certain incompatibility between the content and the method of treatment. A misty island is more effective than a London dinner party as the setting for a novel of indirect philosophic suggestion, and as a result qualities of Virginia Woolf's writing which in her other works tend to appear if not as faults at least as of doubtful appropriateness, are seen in this work to their fullest advantage. In *To the Lighthouse* Virginia Woolf found a subject that enabled her to do full justice to her technique.

5. TIME, CHANGE AND PERSONALITY

ORLANDO, WHICH FOLLOWED *TO THE LIGHTHOUSE* IN 1928, IS the most lighthearted of Virginia Woolf's novels, which is not to say the book is in any way trivial. It is a biography of the author's friend, Victoria Sackville-West, and is hardly a novel in the strict sense. Nor, for that matter, is it a biography in the strict sense, for Orlando, the hero-heroine, is a symbolic figure who epitomizes the history and background of Virginia Woolf's friend, so that the book is a kind of philosophical biography whose central figure spans the centuries from Elizabethan times to the present day, a figure who changes sex in the course of the book and whose environment, behaviour and literary style alters as the story progresses to correspond with those aspects of Victoria Sackville-West's personal and literary heredity which made her what she was, both biologically and culturally. Told with a zest and a humour which set it in a class by itself among Virginia Woolf's books, *Orlando* reflects its author's interest in the relation of the individual to the flux of history, of the present moment to the stream of time, which we have already noted as a feature of *Mrs. Dalloway* and *To the Lighthouse*. Taking the literary and physical ancestry of her fellow-writer, with all sorts of suggestions from her life and work many of which are bound to be lost on the general reader, Virginia Woolf carries Orlando from the time when, a youth of sixteen at the end of the sixteenth century, he is engaged in writing "Æthelbert: A Tragedy in Five Acts," to "the twelfth stroke of midnight, Thursday, the eleventh of October, Nineteen hundred and Twenty Eight" when, now a mature woman, she has the vision which focusses all her past into a single point. Between this beginning and this conclusion lie a series of picturesque incidents, realistically described yet possessing a complex symbolic meaning, which combine to show the individual creating and created by history, changing, developing, carrying forward the past into the present.

The author's preface is illuminating. "Many friends have helped me in writing this book," she begins. "Some are dead and so illustrious that I scarcely dare name them, yet no one can read or write without being perpetually in the debt of Defoe, Sir Thomas Browne, Sterne, Sir Walter Scott, Lord Macaulay, Emily Brontë, De Quincey, and Walter Pater,—to name the first that come to mind." This is the literary past in virtue of which contemporary writing is what it is (again we see the interest in the relation of the present moment to the flux of experience in general) and it is interesting to see what writers Virginia Woolf singles out as "the first that come to mind" as factors on which modern writing depends. The preface continues with expressions of gratitude for help rendered by friends, scholars, historians, critics, which help us to realize the seriousness with which Virginia Woolf took her job of historical reconstruction. For if the tone of the book is light-hearted and the design is fantastic, it is none the less based on carefully garnered historical material: *Orlando* is full of subtle renderings of literary history and oblique expressions of aspects of earlier English civilization, to say nothing of the more obvious pieces of historical writing which occur at intervals throughout the work. But this is no discursive piece of impressionism: everything is carefully organized so as to develop and elaborate the main theme—the development of the hero-heroine through various phases to become finally the modern writer with a modern sensibility. "Finally" is perhaps the wrong word to use in this connection, for the present is conceived less as the end towards which the past has moved than as one among many possible vantage points from which to observe the ever changing flux of time and experience.

The interested reader can probe for himself into the relation between Victoria Sackville-West's life, ancestry and literary work and the adventures and activities of Orlando. The importance of *Orlando* lies less in this relationship than in the colour and vivacity which pervade the book. Having freed herself from any dependence on a conventional plot sequence or single group of events within a limited period of time, Virginia Woolf is responsible now only to her own imagination, and not to the real world at all. That sense of freedom communicates itself to the reader. There is an exuberant play of the imagination here which lights up the precise scholarship that lies behind the fantasy. Occasionally the author speaks in her own person in a tone of amusement or irony or half-serious comment. And she creates her own conventions as she proceeds.

Yet for all this the book will be remembered not as an integrated unit (for the principle of integration is obscure to the reader who does not possess special knowledge) but for the brilliant writing in individual passages. Her description of the great frost of 1604 is one of her finest pieces of prose writing, and demonstrates convincingly that Virginia Woolf could do more than express meditative reverie, for here are clear, hard colours and a precise imagery:

But while the country people suffered the extremity of want, and the trade of the country was at a standstill, London enjoyed a carnival of the utmost brilliancy. The Court was at Greenwich, and the new King seized the opportunity that his coronation gave him to curry favour with the citizens. He directed that the river, which was frozen to a depth of twenty feet and more for six or seven miles on either side, should be swept, decorated and given all the semblance of a park or pleasure ground, with arbours, mazes, alleys, drinking booths, etc., at his expense. For himself and the courtiers, he reserved a certain space immediately opposite the Palace gates; which, railed off from the public only by a silken rope, became at once the centre of the most brilliant society in England. Great statesmen, in their beards and ruffs, despatched affairs of state under the crimson awning of the Royal Pagoda. Soldiers planned the conquest of the Moor and the downfall of the Turk in striped arbours surmounted by plumes of ostrich feathers. Admirals strode up and down the narrow pathways, glass in hand, sweeping the horizon and telling stories of the north-west passage and the Spanish Armada. Lovers dallied upon divans spread with sables. Frozen roses fell in showers when the Queen and her ladies walked abroad. Coloured balloons hovered motionless in the air. Here and there burnt vast bonfires of cedar and oak wood, lavishly salted, so that the flames were of green, orange, and purple fire. But however fiercely they burnt, the heat was not enough to melt the ice which, though of singular transparency, was yet of the hardness of steel. So clear indeed was it that there could be seen, congealed at a depth of several feet, here a porpoise, there a flounder. Shoals of eels lay motionless in a trance, but whether their state was one of death or merely of suspended animation which the warmth would revive puzzled the philosophers. Near London Bridge, where the river had frozen to a depth of some twenty fathoms, a wrecked wherry boat was plainly visible, lying on the bed of the river where it had sunk last autumn, overladen with apples. The old bumboat woman, who was carrying her fruit to market on the Surrey side, sat there in her plaids and farthingales with her lap full of apples, for all the world as if she were about to serve a customer, though a certain blueness about the lips hinted the truth. 'Twas a sight King James specially liked to look upon, and he would bring a troupe of courtiers to gaze with him. In short, nothing could exceed the brilliancy and gaiety of the scene by day. But it was at night that the carnival was at its merriest. For the frost continued unbroken; the nights were of perfect stillness; the moon and stars blazed with the hard fixity of diamonds, and to the fine music of flute and trumpet the courtiers danced.

Even more effective is the description of the thaw that succeeded the frost, the tempestuous scene being linked very adroitly to the hero's emotional disturbance:

Some blind instinct, for he was past reasoning, must have driven him to take the river bank in the direction of the sea. For when the dawn broke, which it did with unusual suddenness, the sky turning a pale yellow and the rain almost ceasing, he found himself on the banks of the Thames off Wapping. Now a sight of the most extraordinary nature met his eyes. Where, for three months and more, there had been solid ice of such thickness that it seemed permanent as stone, and a whole gay city had been stood on its pavement, was now a race of turbulent yellow waters. The river had gained its freedom in the night. It was as if a sulphur spring (to which view many philosophers inclined) had risen from the volcanic regions beneath and burst the ice asunder with such vehemence that it swept the huge and massy fragments furiously apart. The mere look of the water was enough to turn one giddy. All was riot and confusion. The river was strewn with icebergs. Some of these were as broad as a bowling green and as high as a house; others no bigger than a man's hat, but most fantastically twisted. Now would come down a whole convoy of ice blocks sinking everything that stood in their way. Now, eddying and swirling like a tortured serpent, the river would seem to be hurtling itself between the fragments, and tossing them from bank to bank, so that they could be heard smashing against the piers and pillars. But what was the most awful and inspiring of terror was the sight of the human creatures who had been trapped in the night and now paced their twisting and precarious islands in the utmost agony of spirit. Whether they jumped into the flood or stayed on the ice their doom was certain. Sometimes quite a cluster of these poor creatures would come down together, some on their knees, others suckling their babies. One old man seemed to be reading aloud from a holy book. At other times, and his fate perhaps was the most dreadful, a solitary wretch would stride his narrow tenement alone. As they swept out to sea, some could be heard crying vainly for help, making wild promises to amend their ways, confessing their sins and vowing altars and wealth if God would hear their prayers. Others were so dazed with terror that they sat immovable and silent looking steadfastly before them. One crew of young watermen or post-boys, to judge by their liveries, roared and shouted the lewdest tavern songs, as if in bravado, and were dashed against a tree and sunk with blasphemies on their lips. An old nobleman—for such his furred gown and golden chain proclaimed him—went down not far from where Orlando stood, calling vengeance upon the Irish rebels who, he cried with his last breath, had plotted this devilry. Many perished clasping some silver pot or other treasure to their breasts; and at least a score of poor wretches were drowned by their own cupidity, hurl-

102

ing themselves from the bank into the flood rather than let a gold goblet escape them, or see before their eyes the disappearance of some furred gown. For furniture, valuables, possessions of all sorts were carried away on the icebergs. Among other strange sights was to be seen a cat suckling its young; a table laid sumptuously for a supper of twenty; a couple in bed; together with an extraordinary number of cooking utensils.

The conclusion of this chapter, where Orlando, in the midst of the raging flood, discovers the faithlessness of his Russian mistress, marks the climax of the most brilliantly told episode in the book.

There are passages of almost turgid prose, symbolic statements which overreach themselves and fall into confusion or pretentiousness, lyrical passages which never quite soar to their intended heights; not all the devices are successful, nor are all the incidents as significant to the general reader as Virginia Woolf seems to have supposed they would be. The book, that is to say, has some quite serious faults. But it is an impressive experiment, which the reader should peruse with the surface of his mind, not pondering too deeply as he reads but enjoying the colour and vitality of which the book is full and accepting the conventions and devices employed by the author without pausing to rationalize them. Read thus, *Orlando* is an exciting and arresting work.

After this holiday, Virginia Woolf went back to her main job. Having, in *Mrs. Dalloway* and *To the Lighthouse,* worked out a form and a technique that enabled her to present her type of insight so effectively, one might have expected her to crystallize her methods at this stage and to embark on a series of novels written in the same manner. But a certain restlessness, a dissatisfaction with her own achievements, urged her to further experimentation, and *The Waves,* which appeared in 1931, is as different from the two preceding novels as those novels were from her first two. The fluidity which characterized *Mrs. Dalloway* and *To the Lighthouse,* the quiet and effective mingling of objective event and character's thought stream, the subtle alternation of retrospect and anticipation so as to win free of the limitations of traditional chronological narrative, tended to blur the edge of personality: characters are resolved into their ever changing component parts, and their essential unity is difficult to dissentangle from the multifarious stream of thoughts and impressions in terms of which they are characterized. This is particularly true of the hero of *Jacob's Room;* but both Mrs. Dalloway and Mrs. Ramsay have something of the same indistinctness. That indistinctness is not, of course, a defect in any of these three novels, for it is part of the effect deliberately aimed at by the author, and bound up with that sense of fluidity which she was so anxious to communicate. Yet Virginia Woolf seems to have felt, after *To the Lighthouse,* that in her attempt to present the "transparent envelope" of experience she had not done justice to the reality and significance of individual characters; their impressions were not adequately organized in units, nor was the distinction between the thought process of the author and those of the characters made sufficiently clear. And so in *The Waves* she bases the whole work on the carefully organized impression of a limited number of characters, each of whom is made to present those impressions in a series of stylized monologues.

The result is a curiously artificial piece of work. Virginia Woolf takes six characters—Bernard, Neville, Louis, Susan, Rhoda and Jinny—and makes them paint for us their psychological development and progress throughout their lives in a series of vividly enunciated recitatives in which, at different stages in their development, they reveal their characters with a self-awareness and an objective perfection of phrase that preclude any illusion of realism and establish a species of formalistic fiction which is difficult to parallel in any literature. Between each group of monologues occurring during the same period, Virginia Woolf interposes a short interchapter which takes the form of a description of a seashore scene: these descriptions progress from sunrise to sunset as the characters develop from childhood to old age. Each group of monologues is thus introduced by a set piece of description, and the time of day indicated by the description corresponds to the characters' time of life in the immediately following section of the book.

We first see the six characters when, as young children, they are living together in a house with a large garden that stretches down to the shore, taking lessons from the same governess, working and playing with one another and becoming aware of their own characters as a result of these contacts. Life is just beginning, and the introductory description of the scene is symbolic:

The sun had not yet risen. The sea was indistinguishable from the sky, except that the sea was slightly creased as if a cloth had wrinkles in it. Gradually as the sky whitened a dark line lay on the horizon dividing the sea from the sky and the grey cloth became barred with thick strokes moving, one after another, beneath the surface, following each other, pursuing each other, perpetually.

After a carefully picturesque account of the emergence of the first rays of the rising sun, this opening section concludes:

The light struck upon the trees in the garden, making one leaf transparent and then another. One bird chirped high up; there was a pause; another chirped lower down. The sun sharpened the walls of the house, and rested like the tip of a fan upon a white blind and made a blue finger-print of shadow under the leaf by the bedroom window. The blind stirred slightly, but all within was dim and unsubstantial. The birds sang their blank melody outside.

These set pieces of description, of which there are nine in all, are done in a prose which is rich to the point of luxuriance. Nowhere else in Virginia Woolf's work do we get writing like this, for example:

The girl who had shaken her head and made all the jewels, the topaz, the aquamarine, the water-coloured jewels with sparks of fire in them, dance, now bared her brows and with wide-opened eyes drove a straight pathway over the waves. Their quivering mackerel sparkling was darkened; they massed themselves; their green hollows deepened and darkened and might be traversed by shoals of wandering fish. As they splashed and drew back they left a black rim of twigs and cork on the shore and straws and sticks of wood, as if some light shallop had foundered and burst its sides and the sailor had swum to the land and bounded up the cliff and left his frail cargo to be washed ashore.

The rich picturesqueness of imagery here is in some respects paralleled in some of the sketches of *Monday or*

Tuesday, but the suggestion in these interchapters of the set piece, the somewhat over-elaborated study in descriptive prose, and what might best be called the *solidity* of the writing, contrasts with the more rarified and tenuous quality of her most characteristic prose.

There is indeed throughout this book a certain opaqueness in the writing which differentiates it sharply from *Mrs. Dalloway* and *To the Lighthouse*. Instead of the multicoloured and rapidly shifting streams of consciousness which we are shown in the earlier novels, we get here the set monologue in which each character formalizes his impressions and attitudes into what for Virginia Woolf is quite a rigid piece of prose. The following passage, for example, has a stiffness which disconcerts the reader:

"I will not conjugate the verb," said Louis, "until Bernard has said it. My father is a banker in Brisbane and I speak with an Australian accent. I will wait and copy Bernard. He is English. They are all English. Susan's father is a clergyman. Rhoda has no father. Bernard and Neville are the sons of gentlemen. Jinny lives with her grandmother in London. Now they suck their pens. Now they twist their copy-books, and, looking sideways at Miss Hudson, count the purple buttons on her bodice. Bernard has a chip in his hair. Susan has a red look in her eyes. Both are flushed. But I am pale; I am neat, and my knickerbockers are drawn together by a belt with a brass snake. I know the lesson by heart. I know more than they will ever know. I know my cases and my genders; I could know everything in the world if I wished. But I do not wish to come to the top and say my lesson. My roots are threaded, like fibres in a flower pot, round and round about the world. I do not wish to come to the top and live in the light of this great clock, yellow-faced, which ticks and ticks. Jinny and Susan, Bernard and Neville bind themselves into a thong with which to lash me. They laugh at my neatness, at my Australian accent. I will now try to imitate Bernard softly lisping Latin."

107

And though the reader comes to accept this type of artificial monologue as one of the conventions of this kind of writing, it is difficult for him to accept the necessity of the convention.

Even when the sensibility which is expressing itself is timid and individual, the monologue remains solid and formal, the difference in sensibility being marked simply by the images:

"All my ships are white," said Rhoda. "I do not want red petals of hollyhocks or geranium. I want white petals that float when I tip the basin up. I have a fleet now swimming from shore to shore. I will drop a twig in as a raft for a drowning sailor. I will drop a stone in and see bubbles rise from the depths of the sea. Neville has gone and Susan has gone; Jinny is in the kitchen garden picking currants with Louis perhaps. I have a short time alone, while Miss Hudson spreads our copy-books on the schoolroom table. I have a short space of freedom. I have picked all the fallen petals and made them swim. I have put raindrops in some. I will plant a lighthouse here, a head of Sweet Alice. And I will now rock the brown basin from side to side so that my ships may ride the waves. Some will founder. Some will dash themselves against the cliffs. One sails alone. That is my ship.

It is not that there is no subtlety in the character drawing: these six characters as they picture themselves in their monologues emerge as complex and interesting personalities, very carefully conceived. But the author's conception is communicated to us too intellectually, in a series of propositions. We feel that Virginia Woolf is deliberately depriving herself of the use of certain sensitive devices which her earlier work showed her using so effectively. There is no "plot" in the sense that *Mrs. Dalloway* and *To the Lighthouse* possess a plot—a careful patterning of ideas and impressions which enables everything to come together in an extremely complex integration. We see these six characters at different periods in their lives —when they are together as children, then their separation to go to various schools and colleges, their reunion in a London restaurant after college days are over, their divergent paths and attitudes in later life, their final reunion at Hampton Court in middle age—and we are shown, too, their reactions to a seventh character, Percival, who never speaks for himself but who is shown only through the others' eyes. Percival is the normal English Public School type, neither intellectual nor particularly perceptive, but well adjusted and at ease in life, and so a hero to the others. He goes out to India and dies young as a result of a fall from his horse, and the reaction of his six friends to his death helps to characterize them as well as him. The unity of the work consists in the way in which the six develop and fulfil the characters they are seen to possess in childhood. Each runs true to form, and suggestions of maladjustment, poetic temperament, independence or lack of self-confidence are later developed and illustrated as the characters proceed from childhood to old age. At the end Bernard, the best adjusted of the six, the most talkative, the most social, sums up in a long monologue the meaning of it all, looking back on his own past and that of the other five, and concluding with a challenge to the enemy, Death. Yet Bernard's summing up is not really a summing up, for he is simply one of the six, not a figure who is built up so as to include the other five. His conclusions are his own, neither the author's nor the other characters', and Rhoda the timid, Jinny the sensuous, Susan the domestic lover of earth; Louis with his middle-class intelligence and Neville, poetic and dependent—they all disappear without the pattern of their lives being finally interpreted or integrated. Only the suggestion of "the eternal renewal, the incessant rise and fall and fall and rise again," which Bernard expresses towards the end of his final monologue, remains to relate the lives of these six to the recurring sea imagery and the author's final statement, which stands alone at the end of the book:

The waves broke on the shore.

In *The Waves* Virginia Woolf gives up her attempt to reproduce in fiction directly the inarticulate consciousness of her characters—an attempt so characteristic of British and continental fiction of the period—and turns towards a highly formalized rendition of consciousness. In a sense, the characters are speaking through symbolic masks: the idiom is not their own, but one chosen for them by the author as most symbolic of their state of mind. Instead of allowing the various aspects of a character to come together in the course of the book, so that only at the end is the meaning of the character clear and the integration complete, Virginia Woolf has here selected and organized in advance all the thoughts, images, memories which she wants to come together in the mind of each character, and she makes the character come at intervals on to the centre of the stage and deliver in a set speech a collection of these carefully chosen thoughts, images and memories. Each speech therefore possesses the same kind of integration; instead of (as in *Mrs. Dalloway*) the integration becoming apparent as the story proceeds and as the developing meditations of the character become, in the light of what has gone before, cumulatively more significant and more significantly related.

In her search for a technique that would enable her most successfully to communicate her rarified sense of the significant in experience, Virginia Woolf was led, at least once in her career as a novelist, to put into practice a theory which both W. B. Yeats and Eugene O'Neill, at different times and at different stages in their careers, had adopted. This was the theory of the Mask. But the paradox about the Mask is, that though it may be used as a means of conveying suggestions too subtle for more naturalistic means of communication, it is itself so rigid and inflexible that unless you have seen its meaning beforehand you can never be persuaded of it by watching the Mask. The Mask is most effective as a means of communication between those who have the same insights. But Virginia Woolf in her novels tried to convey unique insights. Which explains, perhaps, why *The Waves* is at once the subtlest and the most rigid, the most eloquent and the least communicative, of Virginia Woolf's novels.

With *The Years,* published in 1937, Virginia Woolf returned to what at first sight appears to be a more traditional technique and subject matter. We follow the fortunes of an upper middle-class London family from 1880 to "the present day," noting how the generations grow old one after the other, and the steady march of the years carries with it the fate both of individuals and of the society in which they move. But, superficial resemblance though there may be between *The Years* and a work like *The Forsyte Saga,* the difference between the two is far

111

more striking. Virginia Woolf is not interested in chronicling the decline of a class, or in the differences between succeeding generations: her interest is still centred on her old theme, the flux of experience, life as a fluid mixture of retrospect and anticipation, so that the real subject of *The Years* is precisely what the title would indicate—the years, and the way their passage builds up, embryonically as it were, a transparent envelope which determines the nature and the limits of each individual consciousness. The Pargiter family, from Colonel Abel waiting for his wife to die in 1880, to his children, grown old in the 1930's, simultaneously summing up their past and interrogating their future, constitute a unity and yet a diversity, like the disparate and individually experienced moments of time which nevertheless flow inevitably into a single stream in which past and present condition and indeed constitute each other, so that memory is the faculty which makes life real.

There is nothing startling in the technique of this novel. Conversation is reported in the usual fashion, thought processes are indicated indirectly in the third person and the direction of the thought is made clear by all the usual signposts and explanatory phrases. There is no obvious sign here of the lyrical flow of *To the Lighthouse* or the complex interweaving of consciousnesses that we find in *Mrs. Dalloway;* nor is there anything of the formal monologue of *The Waves*. Yet *The Years* does not mark a reversion to tradition. The experiments, both successful and unsuccessful, had not been in vain; Virginia Woolf had by now achieved a control over words that enabled her, at this late stage in her career, to convey her unique sensibility by sheer luminosity of language. She does not need to depend any more on the patterns of *Mrs. Dalloway* or the symbolic structure of *To the Lighthouse:* she feels free at last to take a simple, chronological sequence and convey into it all that subtle sense of significance, simply by the quality of the writing. There is a plastic handling of language here which is most impressive.

The opening passage—describing a London Spring in 1880—is as good as any to choose as an example:

It was an uncertain spring. The weather, perpetually changing, sent clouds of blue and of purple flying over the land. In the country farmers, looking at the fields, were apprehensive; in London umbrellas were opened and then shut by people looking up at the sky. But in April such weather was to be expected. Thousands of shop assistants made that remark, as they handed neat parcels to ladies in flounced dresses standing on the other side of the counter at Whiteley's and the Army and Navy Stores. Interminable processions of shoppers in the West end, of business men in the East, paraded the pavements, like caravans perpetually marching,—so it seemed to those who had any reason to pause, say, to post a letter, or at a club window in Piccadilly. The stream of landaus, victorias and hansom cabs was incessant; for the season was beginning. In the quieter streets musicians doled out their frail and for the most part melancholy pipe of sound, which was echoed, or parodied, here in the trees of Hyde Park, here in St. James's by the twitter of sparrows and the sudden outbursts of the amorous but intermittent thrush. The pigeons in the squares shuffled in the tree tops, letting fall a twig or two, and crooned over and over again the lullaby that was always interrupted. The gates at the Marble Arch and Apsley House were blocked in the afternoon by ladies in many-coloured dresses wearing bustles, and by gentlemen in frock coats carrying canes, wearing carnations. Here came the Princess, and as she passed hats were lifted. In the basements of the long avenues of the residential quarters servant girls in cap and apron prepared tea. Deviously ascending

113

from the basement the silver teapot was placed on the table, and virgins and spinsters with hands that had staunched the sores of Bermondsey and Hoxton carefully measured out one, two, three, four spoonfuls of tea. When the sun went down a million little gaslights, shaped like the eyes in peacocks' feathers, opened in their glass cages, but nevertheless broad stretches of darkness were left on the pavement. The mixed light of the lamps and the setting sun was reflected equally in the placid waters of the Round Pond and the Serpentine. Diners-out, trotting over the Bridge in hansom cabs, looked for a moment at the charming vista. At length the moon rose and its polished coin, though obscured now and then by wisps of cloud, shone out with serenity, with severity, or perhaps with complete indifference. Slowly wheeling, like the rays of a searchlight, the days, the weeks, the years passed one after another across the sky.

This plastic, effortless prose, with its supple rhythms and easy flow, is writing at its most civilized. It is pregnant with consciousness, yet subtly so; giving nothing away except the *sense* of significance. There is no crude statement of implications; they lie behind the images and the rhythms. This is the sort of thing, we feel, that Henry James really meant to write when he penned a passage like this:

The smoking room at Summersoft was on the scale of the rest of the place—high, light, commodious, and decorated with such refined old carvings and moldings that it seemed rather a bower for ladies who should sit at work at fading crewels than a parliament of gentlemen smoking strong cigars. The gentlemen mustered there in considerable force on the Sunday evening, collecting mainly at one end, in front of one of the cool, fair fireplaces of white marble, the entablature of which was adorned with a delicate little Italian "subject." There was another in the wall that faced it, and, thanks to the mild summer night, a fire in neither; but a nucleus for aggregation was furnished on one side by a table in the chimney corner laden with bottles, decanters, and tall tumblers. Paul Overt was a faithless smoker; he would puff a cigarette for reasons with which tobacco had nothing to do. This was particularly the case on the occasion of which I speak; his motive was the vision of a little direct talk with Henry St. George. The "tremendous" communion of which the great man had held out hopes to him earlier in the day had not yet come off, and this saddened him considerably, for the party was to go its several ways immediately after breakfast on the morrow. He had, however, the disappointment of finding that apparently the author of *Shadowmere* was not disposed to prolong his vigil. He wasn't among the gentlemen assembled when Paul entered, nor was he one of those who turned up, in bright habiliments, during the next ten minutes.

There is an aeration in the former passage which the latter lacks, an absence of self-consciousness in the choice of images and analogies, a sense of complete familiarity with the English language.

From Virginia Woolf's prose at this stage there emanates a conviction that the reader will understand, that he is sensitive and civilized and can adjust his sensibility easily to the author's vision, however unique that may be. We find nothing of this in the great nineteenth century novelists, in Scott or Dickens or Thackeray, none of this sense of equality with the reader (an aesthetic equality, not a community of attitude: the latter belongs more to the older writers). Put the passage from *The Years* already quoted beside this from Scott, and the point becomes clear at once:

It was towards the close of a summer's evening, during the anxious period which we have commemorated, that a young gentleman of quality, well mounted and armed, and accompanied by two servants, one of whom led a sumpter horse, rode slowly up

115

one of those steep passes, by which the Highlands are accessible from the Lowlands of Perthshire. Their course had lain for some time along the banks of a lake, whose deep waters reflected the crimson beams of the western sun. The broken path which they pursued with some difficulty, was in some places shaded by ancient birches and oak-trees, and in others overhung by fragments of huge rock. Elsewhere, the hill, which formed the northern side of this beautiful sheet of water, arose in steep, but less precipitous acclivity, and was arrayed in heath of the darkest purple. In the present times, a scene so romantic would have been judged to possess the highest charms for the traveller; but those who journey in days of doubt and dread, pay little attention to picturesque scenery.

The master kept, as often as the wood permitted, abreast of one or both of his domestics, and seemed earnestly to converse with them, probably because the distinctions of rank are readily set aside among those who are made to be sharers of common danger. The dispositions of the leading men who inhabit this wild country, and the probability of their taking part in the political convulsions that were soon expected, were the subjects of their conversation.

It is not being urged that Virginia Woolf's prose is, abstractedly considered, *better* than that of these older writers; simply that it possesses a quality, not found in the others, which makes it peculiarly appropriate for the kind of purpose for which she employed it—the communication of certain glimmering insights into experience conceived as a "luminous halo."

So in *The Years* the author takes us through the years from episode to episode in the lives of the Pargiters and their circle, from 1880 to 1891, 1907, 1908, 1910, 1911, 1913, 1914, 1917, and "the present day." There is no "plot" in the traditional sense; the moments of crisis are moments of intense awareness of the present and its relation to the past, moments of retrospect, moments when the consciousness suddenly expands to include the past as the essence of the present. The writing is so effective that the whole sum of the book becomes evident from a careful reading of any single passage. In such a work structure is almost unnecessary. The book spans the generations Virginia Woolf herself had known, and comes to an end with the moment of writing. The beginning and end are thus determined by an almost casual factor; but that does not matter, for the luminous writing illuminates as it moves. Even the picture of a London semi-slum is impregnated with that subtle sense of significance that distinguishes it from a Dickensian picture, which in other respects it quite surprisingly resembles:

A voice pealed out across the street, the voice of a woman singing scales.

"What a dirty," he said, as he sat still in the car for a moment —here a woman crossed the street with a jug under her arms— "sordid," he added, "low-down street to live in." He cut off his engine; got out, and examined the names on the door. Names mounted one above another; here on a visiting-card, here engraved on brass—Foster; Abrahamson; Roberts; S. Pargiter was near the top, punched on a strip of aluminum. He rang one of the many bells. No one came. The woman went on singing scales, mounting slowly. The mood comes, the mood goes, he thought. He used to write poetry; now the mood had come again as he stood there waiting. He pressed the bell two or three times sharply. But no one answered. Then he gave the door a push; it was open. There was a curious smell in the hall; of vegetables cooking; and the oily brown paper made it dark. He went up the stairs of what had once been a gentleman's residence. The bannisters were carved; but they had been daubed over with some cheap yellow varnish. He mounted slowly and stood on the landing, uncertain which door to knock at. He was always finding himself now out-

side the doors of strange houses. He had a feeling that he was
no one and nowhere in particular. From across the road came the
voice of the singer deliberately ascending the scale, as if the notes
were stairs; and here she stopped indolently, languidly, flinging
out the voice that was nothing but pure sound. Then he heard
somebody inside, laughing.

We have said that in such a book structure is almost unnecessary—almost, but, of course, not quite. The episodes
which develop one by one as the book proceeds are necessary not only as indicating the cumulative nature of experience, but as describing the original events about which
memory later hovers. Episodes in the childhood of the
Pargiter children are described in the beginning of the
book, and they reappear later on, when the children are
middle-aged or old, as part of the texture of their consciousness.

The descriptions of the scene and the weather which
open each chapter have little of the rich pictorial quality
of the interchapters in *The Waves,* and for that reason
they are perhaps more effective. Description and interpretation do not alternate, as in *The Waves,* but occur simultaneously:

The Autumn wind blew over England. It twitched the leaves
off the trees, and down they fluttered, spotted red and yellow,
or sent them floating, flaunting in wide curves before they settled. In towns coming in gusts round the corners, the wind blew
here a hat off; there lifted a veil high above a woman's head.
Money was in brisk circulation. The streets were crowded. Upon
the sloping desks of the offices near St. Paul's, clerks paused with
their pens on the ruled page. It was difficult to work after the
holidays. Margate, Eastbourne and Brighton had bronzed them
and tanned them. The sparrows and starlings, making their dis-
cordant chatter round the eaves of St. Martin's, whitened the heads

of the sleek statues holding rods or rolls of paper in Parliament Square. Blowing behind the boat train, the wind ruffled the channel, tossed the grapes in Provence, and made the lazy fisher boy, who was lying on his back in his boat in the Mediterranean, roll over and snatch a rope.

But in England, in the North, it was cold. Kitty, Lady Lasswade, sitting on the terrace beside her husband and his spaniel, drew the cloak round her shoulders. She was looking at the hill top, where the snuffer-shaped monument raised by the old Earl made a mark for ships at sea. There was mist on the woods. Near at hand the stone ladies on the terrace had scarlet flowers in their urns. Thin blue smoke drifted across the flaming dahlias in the long beds that went down to the river. "Burning weeds," she said aloud. Then there was a tap on the window, and her little boy in a pink frock stumbled out, holding his spotted horse.

The transition from character to character is done with less careful dovetailing than we find in *Mrs. Dalloway*. The author moves from character to character as she sees fit, and we follow her without any sense of abruptness, carried on easily by the athletic diction. And the conclusion is not as specific or as symbolic as in most of her earlier novels, for the even texture of the work has made this less necessary. The symbolic note is there at the end, but it is a quiet re-statement of what episode after episode has already suggested:

"Aren't they lovely?" said Delia, holding out the flowers.
Eleanor started.
"The roses? Yes . . ." she said. But she was watching the cab. A young man had got out; he paid the driver. Then a girl in a tweed travelling suit followed him. He fitted his latch-key to the door. "There," Eleanor murmured, as he opened the door and they stood for a moment on the threshold. "There!" she repeated as the door shut with a little thud behind them.

Then she turned round into the room. "And now?" she said,

looking at Morris, who was drinking the last drops of a glass of wine. "And now?" she asked, holding out her hands to him.

The sun had risen, and the sky above the houses wore an air of extraordinary beauty, simplicity and peace.

The movement from past to future continues as the book closes.

In a sense, *The Years* is a repetitious book. The very quality of the writing makes its length unnecessary. The full meaning has been there for quite a long time before the book comes to a close. 1917 is as good a date as 1937 for completing the recurring cycle. Indeed, each day is a microcosm of all life, as Virginia Woolf demonstrated so brilliantly in *Mrs. Dalloway*. Put beside *Mrs. Dalloway* or *To the Lighthouse, The Years* appears to have an unnecessary expansion. Is a novel as good if increase of insight stops somewhere about the middle as it is when the insight continues until it ultimately floods the reader at the final resolution? This seems a reasonable criterion to apply, and by it *The Years* appears as a less adequate novel than the two masterpieces of her middle period. Yet if we read it throughout with continuous pleasure, as the sensitive reader undoubtedly does, in what sense is the defect a real one? Perhaps it is possible to distinguish between the kinds of pleasure with which we read such works: the pleasure in reading *The Years* derives more from a recognition of virtuosity, let us say, than from our complete domination by the novel as an integrated work of art.

In no other novel has Virginia Woolf so completely demonstrated her status as a Londoner. Like *Mrs. Dalloway*, this is essentially a London novel, and it is much more a

London novel than the earlier one, for in *The Years* we have London in all its phases and through a period of fifty years. No other modern writer has given such a convincing rendering of the atmosphere of London as it impresses the refined sensibility of a middle-class intellectual. London could always seduce her into the betrayal of a lyrical feeling about the city that is not always strictly relevant to her theme: which may be the explanation of the apparent paradox, that *To the Lighthouse,* perhaps her best novel, is the one farthest removed in setting and atmosphere from city life or its influence.

Virginia Woolf's next, and last, novel, *Between the Acts,* appeared posthumously in the early autumn of 1941. It was completed, though not finally revised, at the time of her death in March. Written under the shadow of war and finished in the midst of it, this book seems to be, in one of its aspects at least, a deliberate attempt to interpret and symbolize the whole process of English living as it had developed through history into the present. The familiar theme of the relation of time and change to personality and experience is this time applied specifically to the English scene. The book is a lyrical tragedy whose hero is England. The setting is not London this time, but a more permanent epitome of the country, the village, where history is more tenacious. "From an aeroplane . . . you could still see, plainly marked, the scars made by the Britons; by the Romans; by the Elizabethan manor house; and by the plough, when they ploughed the hill to grow wheat in the Napoleonic wars." The action revolves around the annual village pageant, which takes the form of a series of scenes expressing the development of English civilization from the beginning, when England was

> A child new born,
> Sprung from the sea
> Whose billows blown by mighty storm
> Cut off from France and Germany
> This isle,

through the Elizabethan age, the "age of reason" and the Victorian age to the present moment in June, 1939, the last being represented by mirrors held up on the stage so that the audience could see themselves reflected while an anonymous voice, braying through a megaphone, informed them that they were "orts, scraps and fragments." At the conclusion, the fragments of the present are integrated through music, a tune played on the gramophone:

> The tune began; the first note meant a second; the second a third. Then down beneath a force was born in opposition; then another. On different levels they diverged. On different levels ourselves went forward; flower gathering some on the surface; others descending to wrestle with the meaning; but all comprehending; all enlisted. The whole population of the mind's immeasurable profundity came flocking; from the unprotected, the unskinned; and dawn rose; and azure; from chaos and cacophony measure; but not the melody of surface sound alone controlled it; but also the warring battle-plumed warriors straining asunder: To part? No. Compelled from the ends of the horizon; recalled from the edge of appalling crevasses; they crashed; solved; united.

Thus the disparate fragments are unified, the separate moments of history are united, and the English village, reaching back into the remote past from this June day in 1939, illustrates how all reality depends on change, all unity on diversity. And that the reality for England is represented as a tragic one, no careful reader of the book can doubt. History flowering into the present is no story of happy fulfilment of heroic promise: the past has made the present fragmentary and the present has made the past petty.

The theme is reiterated in many different ways. As the book opens, the characters are discussing the new cesspool, and "the site they had chosen for the cesspool was . . . on the Roman road." The function of the pageant is to raise funds to install electric light in the old church. Old Mrs. Swithin had been reading an outline of history and "had spent the hours between three and five thinking of rhododendron forests in Piccadilly; when the entire continent, not then, she understood, divided by a channel, was all one; populated, she understood, by elephant-bodied, seal-necked, heaving, surging, slowly writhing, and, she supposed, barking monsters; the iguanodon, the mammoth, and the mastodon; from whom presumably, she thought, we descend." At the end of the book, when the day is done and she is about to go to bed, she takes up her Outline of History again: "Prehistoric man," she read, "half-human, half-ape, roused himself from his semi-crouching position and raised great stones." In the middle of the pageant aeroplanes drone ominously overhead. The minds of the principal characters are full of memories and shifting fancies.

As in *Mrs. Dalloway*, the action takes place in a single day. Pointz Hall, a middle-sized country house, and its immediate environs, provide the scene. Here the Olivers —Giles Oliver and his wife Isa, his father Bartholomew Oliver of the Indian Civil Service, retired, and Bartholomew's sister the widowed Mrs. Swithin—live; Giles, a

London stockbroker who would have liked to be a gentle-man farmer, coming only for the week-ends. The Olivers had been there "only something over a hundred and twenty years"; but there is a portrait of "an ancestress of sorts" hanging at the top of the principal staircase. Isa's mind is running over with original poetic phrases (her poetic character providing, in part, the probability for the lyrical mood of the book). Giles is resentful today, not in the best of tempers. His father, with an old man's waver-ing sensibility, mutters quotations from the poets and pre-serves a proper outward behaviour. Mrs. Swithin thinks of history and her own past. The Olivers' two visitors, who dropped in to lunch and stay for the pageant, are the flamboyant and man-hunting Mrs. Manresa, who for a time arouses Giles's lust, and her companion, William Dodge, maladjusted, poetic, nervous. Miss La Trobe, the obscure character who wrote and designed the pageant and was rumoured to have led a varied and not wholly respectable life, remains behind the scenes tortured with all the frustrations of an artist who has tried to communi-cate a vision to a public who cannot see, and ends the day at the village pub. When the pageant, which is mostly in verse (Miss La Trobe's) is over, and the audience dis-persed, Mr. and Mrs. Giles Oliver finally face each other alone for the first time that day. "Then the curtain rose. They spoke." The unity which the pageant had imposed on all these separate individuals is shattered again, and each turns to his own role. For a brief while each partakes in the lyrical tragedy of English history, and then steps back into his own little drama.

Between the Acts is the most purely symbolical of all

Virginia Woolf's works. The characters' thoughts are less "in character" than symbolically appropriate. The conversation is shifted deliberately from point to point, the interest centering on the symbolic pattern that emerges rather than on naturalistic fidelity:

> "And what did you think of the play?" she asked.
> Bartholomew looked at his son. His son remained silent.
> "And you Mrs. Swithin?" Mrs. Manresa pressed the old lady.
> Lucy mumbled, looking at the swallows.
> "I was hoping you'd tell me," said Mrs. Manresa. "Was it an old play? Was it a new play?"
> No one answered.
> "Look!" Lucy exclaimed.
> "The birds?" said Mrs. Manresa, looking up.
> There was a bird with a straw in its beak; and the straw dropped.
> Lucy clapped her hands. Giles turned away. She was mocking him as usual, laughing.
> "Going?" said Bartholomew. "Time for the next act?"
> And he heaved himself up from his chair. Regardless of Mrs. Manresa and of Lucy, off he strolled too.
> "Swallow, my sister, O sister swallow," he muttered, feeling for his cigar case, following his son.

This has more the quality of a symbolist lyric than of dialogue in a work of fiction. The pageant itself, with its epitomizing of periods in skilful imitation of older literary and conversational styles and its free use of all kinds of visual and verbal symbol, is the key to the method of the book as a whole.

There are little personal dramas played out between the acts of the greater drama of English history, though every character except Mrs. Manresa (who is not English) is caught up in the major play at some point or other. Isa Oliver might be called the heroine of the minor drama.

125

She has not, nor is she meant to have, the psychological reality of Mrs. Dalloway or Mrs. Ramsay. Her fluent poetic fancy runs through the book, suggestive, symbolic, lyrical: it is not "stream of consciousness"; as such it would be improbable and unconvincing. It is a device half-way between the monologues and the interchapters of *The Waves*, which enables the author to use her characters as actors and chorus at the same time. This device establishes a new kind of probability for fiction, more lyrical than narrative: it is implied in the sketches of *Monday or Tuesday* and here first exploited to the full:

"Now may I pluck," Isa murmured, picking a rose, "my single flower. The white or the pink? And press it so, twixt thumb and finger. . . ."

She looked among the passing faces for the face of the man in grey. There he was for one second; but surrounded, inaccessible. And now vanished.

She dropped her flower. What single, separate leaf could she press? None. Nor stray by the beds alone. She must go on; and she turned in the direction of the stable.

"Where do I wander?" she mused. "Down what draughty tunnels? Where the eyeless wind blows? And there grows nothing for the eye. No rose. To issue where? In some harvestless dim field where no evening lets fall her mantle; nor sun rises. All's equal there. Unblowing, ungrowing are the roses there. Change is not; nor the mutable and lovable; nor greetings nor partings; nor furtive findings and feelings, where hand seeks hand and eye seeks shelter from the eye."

She had come into the stable yard where the dogs were chained; where the buckets stood; where the great pear tree spread its ladder of branches against the wall. The tree, whose roots went beneath the flags, was weighted with hard green pears. Fingering one of them she murmured: "How am I burdened with what they drew from the earth; memories; possessions. This is the burden

126

that the past laid on me, last little donkey in the long caravanserai crossing the desert. 'Kneel down,' said the past. 'Fill your pannier from our tree. Rise up, donkey. Go your way till your heels blister and your hoofs crack.' "

The pear was hard as stone. She looked down at the cracked flags beneath which the roots spread. "That was the burden," she mused, "laid on me in the cradle; murmured by waves; breathed by restless elm trees; crooned by singing women; what we must remember: what we would forget."

The lyrical and narrative devices are used boldly in immediate juxtaposition. They do not contradict each other, because the language of the narrative itself is so finely organized, so poetically ordered, that it prepares the reader for these transitions to a purely lyrical organization. Such a passage as that which opens the book prepares equally for a purely symbolic and for a narrative development, and this base of "inclusive" prose (arousing expectations that sanction both a lyrical and a narrative probability) is used to open and close the book, as well as for transitional passages. Here, for example, is the opening:

It was a summer's night and they were talking, in the big room with the windows open to the garden, about the cesspool. The county council had promised to bring water to the village, but they hadn't.

Mrs. Haines, the wife of the gentleman farmer, a goosefaced woman with eyes protruding as if they saw something to gobble in the gutter, said affectedly: "What a subject to talk about on a night like this!"

Then there was silence; and a cow coughed; and that led her to say how odd it was, as a child, she had never feared cows, only horses. But, then, as a small child in a perambulator, a great cart-horse had brushed within an inch of her face. Her family, she told the old man in the arm-chair, had lived near Liskeard

127

for many centuries. There were the graves in the churchyard to prove it.

A bird chuckled outside. "A nightingale?" asked Mrs. Haines. No, nightingales didn't come so far north. It was a daylight bird, chuckling over the substance and succulence of the day, over worms, snails, grit, even in sleep.

And here is the conclusion:

The old people had gone up to bed. Giles crumpled the newspaper and turned out the light. Left alone together for the first time that day, they were silent. Alone, enmity was bared; also love. Before they slept, they must fight; after they had fought, they would embrace. From that embrace another life might be born. But first they must fight, as the dog fox fights with the vixen, in the heart of darkness, in the fields of night.

Isa let her sewing drop. The great hooded chairs had become enormous. And Giles too. And Isa too against the window. The window was all sky without colour. The house had lost its shelter. It was night before roads were made, or houses. It was the night that dwellers in caves had watched from some high place among rocks.

Then the curtain rose. They spoke.

Yet this technique is not altogether successful, for meanings overlap and spill, and the vision is not contained, complex yet whole, within the covers of the book as it is in *Mrs. Dalloway* or *To the Lighthouse*. Is it that the threat of war and destruction, which it does not take too sensitive an eye to see in the background (it emerges in the thoughts of Giles), has complicated the vision beyond expression? We are told that Virginia Woolf was dissatisfied with the work on its completion. Did she brood over it because she felt the pattern had got out of control? In all her other novels (except, perhaps, *The Waves*) there is a real resolution, bringing together all the separate visions and single moments of experience into a single fluid pattern. The suicide of Septimus Warren Smith completed the design of Mrs. Dalloway's experience; and the party that landed by the lighthouse at the moment when Lily Briscoe had her vision and finished her painting interpreted retrospectively the life of Mrs. Ramsay and brought all these lives into a single, developing significance. But in this final work we end "between the acts." The book closes on a rising curtain. Life is too complicated to express in a novel.

An unsympathetic critic would say that at the end of Virginia Woolf's life her vision failed her: in spite of everything, she could not find a method for encompassing all experience as she finally saw it. But if this is true, the cause is not a too limited art but an unlimited ambition. Virginia Woolf set out to distil life into an essence. The more we know about life the less certain we are that it can be so distilled. If it can, perhaps music rather than literature is the art that can do it: it is at least significant that the final comment on the pageant is made not by a speech or a tableau, but by music—"was it Bach, Handel, Beethoven, Mozart, or nobody famous, but merely a traditional tune?"

6. THE UNCOMMON READER

SOME OF VIRGINIA WOOLF'S BEST PROSE IS TO BE FOUND IN her critical essays, which she produced at fairly regular intervals throughout her literary career. The two collections which she entitled *The Common Reader* (first series, 1925; second series, 1932) give a very adequate cross-section of her work in this field. Most of the individual essays which make up these volumes had appeared separately in various periodicals, including the *Times Literary Supplement, Dial, Life and Letters,* and *The Nation,* in England, and the *New York Herald* and the *Yale Review* in the United States. Their collection into two volumes meant that Virginia Woolf took herself seriously as a critic, and the popularity of the books meant that the public did so, too.

To say that Virginia Woolf took herself seriously as a critic is not to imply that her critical work is in any way pretentious, but simply that she was keenly interested in literary criticism and indulged her talent for it freely and confidently. The very title that she chose—"The Common

Reader"—indicates that as a critic she regarded herself as something of an amateur. The motto is from Johnson's life of Gray: ". . . I rejoice to concur with the common reader; for by the common sense of readers, uncorrupted by literary prejudices, after all the refinements of subtlety and the dogmatism of learning, must be generally decided all claim to poetical honours." Virginia Woolf's claim to be Dr. Johnson's common reader is somewhat over-modest: she was certainly much more learned and much more sensitive than that character as Johnson conceived him. Her own conception of the common reader is rather different from the learned doctor's, as we gather from her remarks in the preface to the first series:

> The common reader, as Dr. Johnson implies, differs from the critic and the scholar. He is worse educated, and nature has not gifted him so generously. He reads for his own pleasure rather than to impart knowledge or correct the opinions of others. Above all, he is guided by an instinct to create for himself, out of whatever odds and ends he can come by, some kind of whole—a portrait of a man, a sketch of an age, a theory of the art of writing. He never ceases, as he reads, to run up some rickety and ramshackle fabric which shall give him the temporary satisfaction of looking sufficiently like the real object to allow of affection, laughter, and argument. Hasty, inaccurate, and superficial, snatching now this poem, now that scrap of old furniture without caring where he finds it or of what nature it may be so long as it serves his purpose and rounds his structure, his deficiencies as a critic are too obvious to be pointed out; but if he has, as Dr. Johnson maintained, some say in the final distribution of poetical honours, then, perhaps, it may be worth while to write down a few of the ideas and opinions which, insignificant in themselves, yet contribute to so mighty a result.

This "instinct to create" which Virginia Woolf sees as a characteristic of the common reader is hardly a criterion of amateur criticism in general, but it is a very notable characteristic of her own critical writing. For Virginia Woolf is not a systematic critic, who endeavours to analyze the nature and structure of works of art with a view to assessing each in the light of some general principles. Her aim is to communicate a certain insight about a work, an impression of a writer or of an age, a suggestive or stimulating idea that is adumbrated but never fully developed. Just as in her fiction she is not concerned to create a patterned piece of action whose significance is determined, in the traditional manner, by the rise and fall of clear-cut events, but constructs her novels in order to present as climax the moment of insight, the sudden vision which makes the trivial significant, so in her criticism she avoids the neat statement of theories to be followed by their application to individual cases, and devotes her attention to illustrating, briefly and suggestively, the mood of a writer, the intellectual climate of an age, or some specific problem in a poet's life or work or background.

She does not choose between historical criticism and pure "aesthetic" criticism; she moves freely from one to the other, but is saved from confusion, and from confusing her readers, by her complete awareness, at any given moment, of exactly what she is doing. Some of the sketches are purely biographical or historical, in which she communicates to the reader the feeling of a particular environment. At other times she takes a single point—the nature of the essay, the predicament of modern fiction—and talks round it, suggestively, provocatively, and always interestingly. There is a conversational tone in most of these essays; the author addresses the reader personally, and the prose flows with smoothness and apparent informality.

Her picturesque historical imagination, which served her so well in *Orlando,* is found at its most effective in such an essay as "The Pastons and Chaucer" (*Common Reader,* first series), in which she first tries to give the reader a picture of the kind of life the Pastons lived, and then, setting the work of Chaucer against this background, finds new reasons for Chaucer's work being what it is. Picking out incidents and suggestions from the Paston Letters, she weaves them into a picture of the period:

> For let us imagine, in the most desolate part of England known to us at the present moment, a raw, new-built house, without telephone, bathroom, or drains, arm-chairs or newspapers, and one shelf perhaps of books, unwieldy to hold, expensive to come by. The windows look out upon a few cultivated fields and a dozen hovels, and beyond them there is the sea on one side, on the other a vast fen. A single road crosses the fen, but there is a hole in it, which, one of the farm hands reports, is big enough to swallow a carriage. And, the man adds, Tom Topcroft, the mad bricklayer, has broken loose again and ranges the country half-naked, threatening to kill any one who approaches him. That is what they talk about at dinner in the desolate house, while the chimney smokes horribly, and the draught lifts the carpets on the floor. Orders are given to lock all gates at sunset, and, when the long dismal evening has worn itself away, simply and solemnly, girt about with dangers as they are, these isolated men and women fall upon their knees in prayer.

From such a description she makes an effective transition to Chaucer:

> For sometimes, instead of riding off on his horse to inspect his crops or bargain with his tenants, Sir John would sit, in broad daylight, reading. There, on the hard chair in the comfortless room with the wind lifting the carpet and the smoke stinging his eyes, he would

133

sit reading Chaucer, wasting his time, dreaming—or what strange intoxication was it that he drew from books? Life was rough, cheerless, and disappointing. A whole year of days would pass fruitlessly in dreary business, like dashes of rain on the window pane. . . . But Lydgate's poems or Chaucer's, like a mirror in which figures move brightly, silently, and compactly, showed him the very skies, fields, and people whom he knew, but rounded and complete. Instead of waiting listlessly for news from London or piecing out from his mother's gossip some country tragedy of love and jealousy. here, in a few pages, the whole story was laid before him. And then as he rode or sat at table he would remember some description or saying which bore upon the present moment and fixed it, or some string of words would charm him, and putting aside the pressure of the moment, he would hasten home to sit in his chair and learn the end of the story.

And this provides her with a starting point for a discussion of Chaucer's way of writing, the kind of morality implied in his work, the sort of pleasure one derives from it. This is to discuss Chaucer from a very limited point of view—she is concerned only in discovering what new ideas about Chaucer we can get by considering him as the kind of author read by Sir John Paston "in the comfortless room with the wind blowing and the smoke stinging"— but the very limitations add point and suggestiveness to the remarks: this is an angle from which we have not looked at Chaucer before, and Virginia Woolf makes us look from that angle. We do not see everything from that viewpoint, but what we do see is exciting.

This is Virginia Woolf's method in most of her critical writing. Her criticism has not the consistency or richness of a systematic critic living in a stable civilization: it has neither Dr. Johnson's assurance nor Coleridge's profundity; but it is always illuminating, always fresh, always

honest. Sometimes she simply communicates the substance of a work in a series of carefully organized impressions; and of course the impressions are tendentious, they
are *her* impressions, they are the result of reading the work
in one way only, but she always admits this, and communicates the insight for what it is worth. Or she will take
an idea, and play with it for a certain time before putting
it down, as in her essay "On Not Knowing Greek." Sometimes the point is interesting but not, perhaps, very important, as in her remark about the influence of the climate
on Greek and Roman literature:

> It is the climate that is impossible. If we try to think of Sophocles
> here, we must annihilate the smoke and the damp and the thick wet
> mists. We must sharpen the lines of the hills. We must imagine a
> beauty of stone and earth rather than of woods and greenery. With
> warmth and sunshine and months of brilliant, fine weather, life of
> course is instantly changed; it is transacted out of doors, with the
> result, known to all who visit Italy, that small incidents are debated
> in the street, not in the sitting-room, and become dramatic; make
> people voluble; inspire in them that sneering, laughing, nimbleness
> of wit and tongue peculiar to the Southern races, which has nothing
> in common with the slow reserve, the low half-tones, the brooding
> introspective melancholy of people accustomed to live more than
> half the year indoors.

Gradually, as the idea is held up and turned round,
further points are suggested, generalizations about literature or life which often help us to understand her own
problems and methods as a novelist:

> Yet in a play how dangerous this poetry, [she is talking of Greek
> drama] this lapse from the particular to the general must of neces-
> sity be, with the actors standing there in person, with their bodies
> and their faces passively waiting to be made use of! . . . The in-
> tolerable restrictions of the drama could be loosened, however, if a

135

means could be found by which what was general and poetic, comment, not action, could be freed without interrupting the movement of the whole. It is this that the choruses supply; the old men or women who take no active part in the drama, the undifferentiated voices who sing like birds in the pauses of the wind; who can comment, or sum up, or allow the poet to speak himself or supply, by contrast, another side to his conception. Always in imaginative literature, where characters speak for themselves and the author has no part, the need of that voice is making itself felt. For though Shakespeare . . . dispensed with the chorus, novelists are always devising some substitute—Thackeray speaking in his own person, Fielding coming out and addressing the world before his curtain rises. So to grasp the meaning of the play the chorus is of the utmost importance. One must be able to pass easily into those ecstasies, those wild and apparently irrelevant utterances, those sometimes obvious and commonplace statements, to decide their relevance or irrelevance, and give them their relation to the play as a whole.

And then the scope is contracted again, and we get a single point made:

Further, in reckoning the doubts and difficulties [of reading Greek] there is this important problem— Where are we to laugh in reading Greek? There is a passage in the *Odyssey* where laughter begins to steal upon us, but if Homer were looking we should probably think it better to control our merriment. To laugh instantly it is almost necessary (though Aristophanes may supply us with an exception) to laugh in English. . . . Thus humour is the first of the gifts to perish in a foreign tongue, and when we turn from Greek to Elizabethan literature it seems, after a long silence, as if our great age were ushered in by a burst of laughter.

Her criticism is impressionist in a sense, but in the best sense. She does not, as so many critics have done, confuse autobiography with criticism, but notes certain responses she has had to books and authors and tries to discover what it was in the work or the author that accounts for those responses. The answer may be given in historical or psychological terms; she may give the reader a picture of the writer's environment or discuss some aspects of his personal life; or the answer may be more purely critical, dwelling on the way Sidney constructed his sentences; or it may be both, as when she relates Sir Thomas Browne's style to his character. Any description of her own responses is always a preliminary to discovering their causes, and according to the point of view she adopts for the moment the causes can be of many different kinds. She saves herself from dogmatism by never suggesting that her account gives the whole cause: she is simply discussing one causal factor which interests her and in which she tries to interest the reader. Every now and again, as in her discussion of the Elizabethan dramatist's view of reality or of the methods of contemporary novelists, she raises a question which is of particular concern to her as a novelist (her discussion of the function of the chorus in Greek drama, already quoted, should be read side by side with *Between the Acts*) and the tone becomes more serious and eloquent.

Frequently in these essays we come across passages in which Virginia Woolf is speaking more as the novelist than as the critic. In writing about Montaigne, she is led to remark on the difficulty of expression:

There is, in the first place, the difficulty of expression. We all indulge in the strange, pleasant process called thinking, but when it comes to saying, even to some one opposite, what we think, then how little we are able to convey! The phantom is through the mind and out of the window before we can lay salt on its tail, or slowly sinking and returning to the profound darkness which it has lit up

137

momentarily with a wandering light. Face, voice, and accent eke out our words and impress their feebleness with character in speech. But the pen is a rigid instrument; it can say very little; it has all kind of habits and ceremonies of its own. It is dictatorial too: it is always making ordinary men into prophets, and changing the natural stumbling trip of human speech into the solemn and stately march of pens.

It is partly her sense of this problem that led her to continual experiment in methods of writing fiction. This, and her sense of the importance of the unique personal vision which it is the duty of the novelist to communicate as effectively as he can, were two of the most important factors in her work as a novelist, and we see them discussed frequently in her criticism. She praises De Quincey for his ability to combine the record of external events with that profounder kind of writing in which "suddenly the smooth narrative parts fly asunder, arch opens beyond arch, the vision of something for ever flying, for ever escaping, is revealed, and time stands still." She defines a masterpiece (in her essay on "Robinson Crusoe," *Second Common Reader*) as a book "where the vision is clear and order has been achieved." We get some insight into the function of poetic reverie and dialogue in *Between the Acts* in her remark that "Verse in the *Arcadia* performs something of the function of dialogue in the modern novel. It breaks up the monotony and strikes a high light." ("The Countess of Pembroke's Arcadia." *Second Common Reader.*)

Perhaps the most effective of all Virginia Woolf's critical writing are those passages in which she sums up the atmosphere of a character or a period. This is not strictly criticism at all, but a species of history. She is particularly

138

fond of taking minor characters whose works are today unread and whose names are almost forgotten, and out of their works (particularly their letters and diaries) weaving together a picture of their way of life, their attitudes, their environment. Her vivid pictures of Geraldine Jewsbury, of Parson Woodforde and the Reverend John Skinner, are not based on any extensive original research, but on the characters' own writings, from which she selects, epitomizes, summarizes, with uncommon skill. As a reviewer she seldom attempted a clear-cut discussion of the nature and value of the work in hand (she did that only when the work clearly reinforced or contradicted the theories implicit in her own practice: to let Galsworthy, for example, get away without some censure would be to endanger her own position, and similarly she praised the early Conrad). She preferred to re-create for the reader the impression which the author had made on her. This is why she excelled as a reviewer of biographical or antiquarian works: she could communicate in a short article the essential meaning of a long biography, summing up the life and character of an individual with vividness and economy. This is to regard the function of a reviewer not as evaluation but as a lively communication of the essence of the book reviewed, which is surely a legitimate point of view.

From the two volumes of *The Common Reader* we get the impression of a wide range of reading and an extraordinary catholicity of taste. The essay on "Robinson Crusoe," a work written from a point of view antithetical to that of Virginia Woolf herself as a novelist, affords perhaps the best evidence of her catholicity, for she describes clearly Defoe's methods and attitude and then proceeds to give him credit for employing them effectively and consistently. The conclusion of this essay (which is to be found in the *Second Common Reader*) is particularly interesting:

> Thus Defoe, by reiterating that nothing but a plain earthenware pot stands in the foreground, persuades us to see remote islands and the solitudes of the human soul. By believing fixedly in the solidity of the pot and its earthiness, he has subdued every other element to his design; he has roped the whole universe into harmony. And is there any reason, we ask as we shut the book, why the perspective that a plain earthenware pot exacts should not satisfy us as completely, once we grasp it, as man himself in all his sublimity standing against a background of broken mountains and tumbling oceans with stars flaming in the sky?

If we grant that Virginia Woolf's critical essays are only rarely criticism in the strict academic sense, we have to concede that they are frequently history, biography, discourse or argument maintained at a high level of intelligence and sensitivity. Leslie Stephen, her father, had called his essays "Hours in a Library," and this title might well have stood for those of his daughter. They are in the same tradition: in both writers the form of the essay is determined by the particular problem under discussion; the method shifts with the subject matter; the individual insight matters more than the systematic presentation of a philosophy; and biography tends to oust criticism. Virginia Woolf differs from her father in that her insights are subtler, her vision more sensitively seen and presented, and she is much more conscious of the difficulty of attaining and communicating awareness of what is significant in experience.

And there is a more important difference. Leslie Stephen was critic, biographer, philosopher, but no creative artist, while his daughter was primarily a sensitive and gifted novelist with a very keen sense of the problems that faced a writer of fiction in her generation. And thus while the bulk of her critical writing is descriptive, evocative, suggestive, occasionally she devotes her whole attention to a consideration of the problems of her craft. And here she writes as a novelist, raising questions which interest her as a practitioner, not merely as a reader. Roughly speaking, it might be said that when she deals with contemporary novelists she writes from the point of view of a fellow writer rather than "the common reader," and when she deals with books and writers of a past age she writes in the manner already described. One of her earliest works of the former type is the paper she read to the Heretics at Cambridge in 1924, entitled *Mr. Bennett and Mrs. Brown,* in which she makes points very similar to those she makes in her *Common Reader* essays on Modern Fiction and on "How It Strikes a Contemporary," to which reference has already been made. *Mr. Bennett and Mrs. Brown* dates from the period during which Virginia Woolf was thinking most furiously about the problems of her art, and as a result it provides one of the clearest examples of how she used criticism of contemporaries as a means of discussing her own position as a creative artist. She divides the twentieth century writers into the Edwardians (including Wells, Bennett, and Galsworthy) and the Georgians (including E. M. Forster, D. H. Lawrence, Lytton Strachey, James Joyce and T. S. Eliot). Both groups would agree that the function of the novelist is primarily to create character—whatever that phrase means. The former group

141

make the mistake of confusing the presentation of character with the description of the material circumstances surrounding the character, while the latter, in just revolt against this practice, are more concerned with destroying these unsatisfactory techniques than with the more positive task of perfecting their own art. Arnold Bennett, whom she appears to admire most of the Edwardian trilogy, wastes his very real gifts through his insistence on the importance of objective detail, and as a result the artist's vision of a complete character is never communicated. It is that vision which Virginia Woolf is most concerned to communicate. She builds up her conception of a woman whom she met in a train and calls Mrs. Brown, and then discusses how she could best communicate this conception. She asked the Edwardians how to do it—

and they said, 'Begin by saying that her father kept a shop in Harrogate. Ascertain the rent. Ascertain the wages of shop assistants in the year 1878. Discover what her mother died of. Describe cancer. Describe calico. Describe—' But I cried, 'Stop! Stop!' And I regret to say that I threw that ugly, that clumsy, that incongruous tool out of the window, for I knew that if I began describing the cancer and the calico, my Mrs. Brown, that vision to which I cling though I know no way of imparting it to you, would have been dulled and tarnished and vanished for ever.

It is essays such as these—by far the smaller part of Virginia Woolf's critical work—that show her evaluating contemporary literature using as a criterion the degree to which these writers were able to see and to solve the problems which she as a novelist felt to be most pressing. They also show how conscious she was of the "intellectual climate" of her own time. She was perfectly aware of the factors in the cultural situation which made Wells, Bennett and Galsworthy write as they did and which impelled writers like Lawrence and Joyce to find other ways. She tells her audience to "tolerate the spasmodic, the obscure, the fragmentary, the failure" because this is a transitional age, coming between the grand confidence of the Victorians and another and (she predicts) even greater age; and a transitional age is bound to be experimental and revolutionary in its culture. She acknowledges that many of the experiments are unsuccessful; many are wholly negative and, while serving a necessary purpose in sweeping away dead conventions, have no positive function. In *A Letter to a Young Poet* (1932) she sympathizes with the predicament of the modern poet, sees the sources of his confusion and his obscurity and admits their necessity, but does not concede that the poetry is therefore good. It has the negative virtue of a destructive vitality, but lacks richness and beauty—qualities that will not come until the young poet ceases to think and write only of himself and his own problems and writes, as Shakespeare did, about people as unlike himself as possible. She adds that while it is the duty of the young poet to experiment as feverishly as possible, it is equally his duty to refrain from publishing these experiments until he has arrived at a stage when publication will no longer be able to check his freedom. To publish prematurely is to "curb the wild torrent of spontaneous nonsense which is now, for a few years only, your divine gift in order to publish prim little books of experimental verse." It is difficult to reconcile this advice with her own publication of *Monday or Tuesday*, but perhaps she felt that it is more important for a poet to be free from the limiting demands of an audience than for a novelist. At any rate, it is in works

143

such as these that Virginia Woolf shows her awareness of the predicament of the artist in her time, her acknowledgement both of the necessity and of the dangers of experimentation. The sense that her own age was a transitional one was fundamental with her, expressed in *Mr. Bennett and Mrs. Brown* with a violence and a simplicity which perhaps later she would have repudiated: "On or about December 1910 human character changed." This statement, and its interesting elaboration, date from the year before the publication of *Mrs. Dalloway,* a book which marked her attainment of maturity as an artist. A consciousness of the cultural transition that was taking place in her own time played a very large part in determining the nature and quality of her work.

No one can read through Virginia Woolf's essays and critical writings without becoming aware of her strong views about the position of her own sex. She believed firmly that women were intellectually the complete equals of men and they have contributed less to culture only because of the conditions under which in almost all civilizations they have been forced to live. She is not much concerned with fighting for women's political rights, but she concentrates her energies on what for her is much more important, the securing of educational and cultural equality for women. Frequent references in her work to the frustration of talent to which women were condemned throughout the ages make it clear that she felt very strongly on this question, and in two papers read at Cambridge in October, 1928 (to the Arts Society at Newnham and the Odtaa at Girton), which she subsequently worked into a single book, *A Room of One's Own,* she developed the point at some length. The

144

substance of her argument is contained in her effective parable of Shakespeare's sister:

Let me imagine, since facts are hard to come by, what would have happened had Shakespeare had a wonderfully gifted sister, called Judith, let us say. . . . She was as adventurous, as imaginative, as agog to see the world as he was. But she was not sent to school. She had no chance of learning grammar and logic, let alone of reading Horace and Virgil. She picked up a book now and then, one of her brother's perhaps, and read a few pages. But then her parents came in and told her to mend the stockings or mind the stew and not to moon about with books and papers. They would have spoken sharply but kindly. . . . Perhaps she scribbled some pages up in an apple loft on the sly, but was careful to hide them or set fire to them. Soon, however, before she was out of her teens, she was to be betrothed to the son of a neighbouring wool-stapler. She cried out that marriage was hateful to her, and for that she was severely beaten by her father. Then he ceased to scold her. He begged her instead not to hurt him, not to shame him in this matter of her marriage. He would give her a chain of beads or a fine petticoat, he said; and there were tears in his eyes. How could she disobey him? How could she break his heart? The force of her own gift alone drove her to it. She made up a small parcel of her belongings, let herself down by a rope one summer's night and took the road to London. The birds that sang in the hedge were not more musical than she was. She had the quickest fancy, a gift like her brother's for the tune of words. Like him, she had a taste for the theatre. She stood at the stage door; she wanted to act, she said. Men laughed in her face. The manager—a fat, loose-lipped man—guffawed. He bellowed something about poodles dancing and women acting—no woman, he said, could possibly be an actress. He hinted—you can imagine what. She could get no training in her craft. Could she even seek her dinner in a tavern or roam the streets at midnight? Yet her genius was for fiction and lusted to feed abundantly upon the lives of men and women and the study of their ways. At last—for she was very young, oddly like Shakespeare the poet in her face, with the same grey eyes and rounded brows—at last Nick Greene the actor-

145

manager took pity on her; she found herself with child by that gentleman and so—who shall measure the heat and violence of the poet's heart when caught and tangled in a woman's body?—killed herself one winter's night and lies buried at some cross-roads where the omnibuses now stop outside the Elephant and Castle.

She concludes with an appeal to her audience—women students at Cambridge—to take advantage of the degree of educational opportunity now afforded to their sex and play their parts independently and courageously so that "the opportunity will come and the dead poet who was Shakespeare's sister will put on the body which she has so often laid down."

In the course of these two lectures Virginia Woolf makes clear that it is not only women who have been denied the possibility of exercising their talents as creative artists: it is true of the whole working class, of every one, indeed, who has not a room of his own and a minimum income. She quotes Sir Arthur Quiller-Couch: "Believe me—and I have spent a great part of ten years in watching some three hundred and twenty elementary schools—we may prate of democracy, but actually, a poor child in England has little more hope than had the son of an Athenian slave to be emancipated in that intellectual freedom of which great writings are born." And again, "The poor poet has not in these days, nor has had for two hundred years, a dog's chance." And she adds: "Intellectual freedom depends upon material things. Poetry depends upon intellectual freedom. And women have always been poor, not for two hundred years merely, but from the beginning of time. Women have had less intellectual freedom than the sons of Athenian slaves. Women, then, have not had a dog's chance of writing poetry. That is why I have laid so much stress on money and a room of one's own." Her feminism is rooted in a larger democratic feeling which is largely concerned with ends and tends to ignore discussion of means. It is the democracy of one who has been born and bred an intellectual aristocrat. All those who have talent should be given the opportunity to develop and use it, should be allowed to have an income and a room of their own; but of those who have neither income, nor room, nor talent, nothing is said. And indeed what could be said?

Most of Virginia Woolf's discussions of the position of her sex are good-humoured though serious. It comes therefore as a surprise to find in what is the most political of all her books a note almost of savagery in her attack on male domination and its effects on civilization. *Three Guineas*, which appeared in 1938, is a series of three essays presented as an answer to an appeal for a contribution by the treasurer of a society to prevent war by protecting culture and intellectual liberty. She begins by pointing out the difference between the writer of the letter, whom she pictures as a middle-aged barrister, and herself, a woman, a member of the sex which has, until very recently, been denied all the opportunities of education, independence and a professional career and which is still denied all but a very limited degree of such opportunities. This is a man's world, its organizations, governments, institutions are run by men: it is the men who cause wars and fight them. After a bitter comparison between the lot of man and of woman in modern civilization, she concludes the first essay by deciding that the first step towards preventing war is to help to improve women's educational opportunities; so as a preliminary she subscribes a guinea to a fund for re-building a women's college. She pursues the argument in the second essay by putting side by side with the original letter a communication from the treasurer of a society to help the daughters of educated men to obtain employment in the professions. After a lengthy discussion of the implications of this juxtaposition, in which the lot of the professional woman is discussed and the paradox of her being asked by a man to contribute some of her new and scanty earnings to his organization is pointed out, Virginia Woolf decides that the next step towards helping to avoid war is to send a guinea to this women's society, on condition that the society "help all properly qualified people, of whatever sex, class or colour, to enter your profession; and further on condition that in the practice of your profession you refuse to be separated from [the traditional feminine virtues of] poverty, chastity of mind [i.e., integrity], derision [i.e., avoidance of self-advertisement] and freedom from unreal loyalties [such as old schools, old churches, old ceremonies]." Having now brought home to the writer of the original letter the position of a professional woman on this matter, she is free to include her feminism in its larger democratic base: she agrees that the monster that tyrannized over women has now enlarged his scope and "is interfering now with your liberty; he is dictating how you shall live; he is making distinctions not merely between the sexes, but between the races." So she finally sends the writer of the original letter her third guinea, because now "the sons and daughters of educated men are fighting side by side" against "the whole iniquity of dictatorship, whether in Oxford or Cambridge, in Whitehall or Downing Street, against Jews or against women, in England, or in Germany, or in Italy or in Spain." The fight for women's rights now appears part of the larger fight for freedom. Yet she will not join the "society for preventing war by defending culture and intellectual freedom." The daughters of educated men could best co-operate in this end by forming a new society—an Outsiders' Society, for women are outside all the military and other traditions to which their brothers and fathers belong. The place of women as she describes it is indeed something like that of the working class as described by Marx—they have no "country" in the sense that the upper-class male patriot has, yet peace and progress are essential to them. With a final elaboration of the injustices suffered by women, chiefly this time during the nineteenth century, she concludes the third essay. She has given three guineas to three different treasurers, but all really to the same cause.

That Virginia Woolf's whole political attitude was coloured by her resentment at the way the male sex had treated the female is perhaps natural in the circumstances. She herself had enjoyed unusual opportunities and had made unusual use of them, but this could only make her the more aware of the restrictions under which most of her sex laboured. The novel had almost been taken over by women during her lifetime—a list of the distinguished women writers of the 1920's is almost a list of the most sensitive and original novelists of the day—and this evidence of what women could do if they were given half a chance amply bore out her contention that it was not natural inferiority but unfair treatment that had limited the literary achievements of her sex in the past. Her critical essays include numerous accounts of women who were inhibited by their sex from developing their talents as writers. Growing up in a predominantly male atmosphere —an intellectual atmosphere of libraries and leather chairs and cigar smoke—she had not become aware of the disabilities under which most of her sex laboured until she looked outside and saw how exceptional her own case was. And even her own case bore sufficient evidence of women's disabilities: surrounded in her childhood by the Victorian great, she must have noticed what a predominantly man's world this world of university men and writers was, and how women entered into it only rarely, by accident or special favour. It did not take much effort to extend the political liberalism that she imbibed in her youth to include the emancipation of women.

In spite of her strong feeling on this matter, Virginia Woolf remained on the whole outside politics, content to justify her position implicitly and unanswerably by her creative work. She was not an "escapist": she was very much aware of contemporary political problems and moved all her life in an environment in which they were continually discussed. But in the main she concerned herself with ends rather than with means, and, while acknowledging the existence and the importance of the world of action, devoted her main energies to what she was most fitted for, the communication of her personal vision. It is doubtful that, with her background and her talents, she could have taken any other course with success—though the force and clarity of much of her occasional prose sometimes make us wonder whether she would not have made a brilliant political pamphleteer. For while in her fiction her prose tends to be subtle and lyrical, elsewhere she can write in a most forthright and virile idiom.

We have already noted Virginia Woolf's interest in biography: much of her criticism is biographical in its approach, and even her discussions of the condition of women are often presented through a biographical sketch of some woman writer or potential writer whose talent was frustrated by the disabilities of her sex. It remains to mention her two full length biographies, the half-humorous, light-hearted biography of Flush, Elizabeth Barrett Browning's spaniel (*Flush*, 1933), and—the last of her books to be published in her lifetime—the careful and sympathetic study of her friend Roger Fry, the art critic (*Roger Fry*, 1940). *Flush*, a short and lively book, has something of the qualities of *Orlando*, though much simpler in design. The life of the dog is reconstructed mostly from Mrs. Browning's letters, and in the course of the biography there are many glimpses of the Brownings, both before and after their marriage. It is a *jeu d'esprit*, carried out with great skill; a perfect thing of its kind.

The biography of Roger Fry, who died in 1934, was not an easy book for Virginia Woolf to write. They had been good friends, and Fry had been a member of that fairly intimate literary and artistic circle in which Virginia Woolf spent so much of her life. It was therefore difficult for her to get sufficiently far away from her subject to be able to see it in proper perspective. As a result the book, though written in a style at once simple and sensitive, lacks that final touch of artistry which the reader expects from her work. Virginia Woolf was very much in sympathy with Roger Fry's views on art, and keenly appreciative of his personality and character. The biography is a sympathetic and unpretentious account of the subject's life, work and ideas. It has none of the stuffiness of conventional biography; it is neither adulatory nor "objective"; it is done with a kind of careful carelessness that is refreshing in a work of this kind. Yet it has little of the light and spirit that a full length biography by Virginia Woolf ought to have possessed. The separate episodes and periods are not fused into an illuminating whole. Virginia Woolf has not here exercised her unique talent for symbolic organization, and the book tends to fall apart; here is a fairly pedestrian list of facts, here a series of quotations from his letters, with running comments, here an account of his philosophy. It may be that her sense of responsibility in writing her friend's life prevented her from viewing it—as she ought to have viewed it—as fiction, as something over which she could let her creative imagination play until the proper insight had been achieved. The book contains some admirable passages; it lights up on occasion in a remarkable way, but the illumination is neither continuous nor richly patterned. An impressive biography, as biographies go, but not revealing the full power of its author's genius. She did better in writing about characters she had never known except through her imagination or in giving a real character the symbolic dimensions of a protagonist in a work of fiction as she did with Mr. Ramsay in *To the Lighthouse*, who is a portrait of her father, Leslie Stephen. And perhaps that is a comment on the nature of her art in general.

152

7. THE SUMMING UP

WHAT, THEN, WAS VIRGINIA WOOLF'S CONTRIBUTION TO ENG-
lish literature? It was a very real, if in some sense a limited,
one. She developed a type of fiction in which sensitive personal reactions to experience can be objectified and patterned in a manner that is both intellectually exciting and
aesthetically satisfying. It is a delicate art. The robustness
that makes itself felt in her criticism and in *Orlando* is not
to be discovered in her characteristic novels, whose function is to distil a significance out of the data discovered by
a personal sensibility and, by projecting that significance
dramatically through the minds of others, to maintain an
unstable equilibrium between lyrical and narrative art.
She achieved that with greatest success in *Mrs. Dalloway*
and *To the Lighthouse*. In the earlier novels the scales
come down too heavily on the side of narrative, with the
result that the lyrical elements are not properly fitted in;
while in *Between the Acts* the scales are weighted on the
lyrical side and the narrative is never wholly justified. *The*

Waves introduces a not quite successful device for carrying on a narrative by means of lyrical monologues, while in *The Years* the reader senses a virtuosity in excess of the novel's requirements. Only in the two middle novels is the precarious balance maintained throughout: only in these is she able to refine life sufficiently to make it fully adaptable to her characteristic treatment.

The Victorian novelist tended on the whole to produce a narrative art whose patterns were determined by a public sense of values. Virginia Woolf, on the other hand, sensitive to the decay of public values in her time, preferred the more exacting task of patterning events in terms of her personal vision, which meant that she had on her hands the additional technical job of discovering devices for convincing the reader, at least during his period of reading, of the significance and reality of this vision. The English novel in the eighteenth and nineteenth centuries was essentially a public instrument; antithetical to lyric poetry. Its function was to utilize the preconceptions of readers in the presentation of a patterned series of events. (Lyrical poetry ignores, as a rule, public preconceptions and endeavours to communicate violently and directly a personal awareness of the poet's.) That the distinction between these two forms of art should be deliberately broken down in the post-Victorian period was only natural, for the distinction between public and private truth in every field was becoming blurred. There were many ways of responding to this situation: that of Virginia Woolf produced a type of art which, at its best, possesses a subtle and fragile beauty that will outlast the more rough-hewn works of many of her contemporaries.

Into the influences that affected her method we need not enter. The important thing is not that Proust or Joyce or any other writer influenced her writing, but that she developed a view of her art which made her susceptible to that kind of influence. Influences are not accepted passively by writers; they are actively embraced, and only when they coincide with the attitude the writer has already come to have: the important thing for the critic is to understand that attitude and its meaning for the writer's art.

It is doubtful whether the work of Virginia Woolf has permanently expanded the art of fiction. Her techniques are not easily isolated or imitated. But an author's greatness is not measured by the extent to which he can be imitated. Virginia Woolf can afford to rest her claims on her novels, which show her to be one of the half-dozen novelists of the present century whom the world will not easily let die. There can be little question that she was the greatest woman novelist of her time, though she herself would have objected to the separation of her sex implied in such a judgment.

Her sudden and tragic death in March, 1941, shocked the public. It was only afterwards that her husband made known some aspects of her life that had hitherto been unguessed even by many of her friends. With all her endowments—perhaps because of them—she had not been free throughout her life from a haunting fear. She was subject to periodic fits of acute depression of which one, in the middle of the first World War, was serious enough to develop into a complete, though fortunately temporary, mental breakdown. Whenever she overworked neurasthenic symptoms appeared, and she was pursued by the dread of insanity. Lively, sociable, and eminently sane in three quarters of her life, she yet knew periods of the darkest despair. She struggled continually against the recurrence of the earlier breakdown. In March, 1941, exhausted after the completion of her new novel and dissatisfied, as she always was on finishing a work, with what she had done, her fear of insanity grew stronger. The strain of the war added its burden: the bombs had completely destroyed the Woolfs' London home and library, and they had moved to a cottage on the eastern edge of the South Downs over which the German bombers roared in from across the Channel. Incendiary bombs fell frequently; neighbours required first-aid and were sometimes beyond it. Virginia Woolf endured all this with outward calm, until early Spring. And then one morning late in March she walked, as she had often done before, across the Downs to the River Ouse. They found her walking stick on the bank.

On the morning of her suicide she wrote two notes, one to her husband Leonard Woolf, and one to her sister Vanessa. "I feel certain," she wrote to her husband, "that I am going mad again. I feel we can't go through another of those terrible times.[1] And I shan't recover this time." She had fought against it, but could fight no longer. Her husband had been "so perfectly good," and she could not go on and spoil his life.

It was a symbolic ending. All her life she had been fas-

[1] Referring to the time of her previous mental breakdown, about twenty-five years before. This sentence was consistently misquoted in the press. The phrase "terrible times" is not a reference to the war; it was certainty of madness, not inability to face the war that drove her to suicide.

cinated by the problem of the flow of time and its relation to experience. Her novels are full of images of flowing water and other symbols of the flux of life. Personality, as she perceived it, was a unity arising out of continual change, consciousness a continual blending of reminiscence and anticipation. When she united herself with the flux of experience by disappearing into the flowing waters of an English river, anyone who had read and appreciated her books must have felt a sense of shock and of almost personal grief; but he would have understood why she chose to end her life in that way.

BIBLIOGRAPHY

BIBLIOGRAPHY

I. VIRGINIA WOOLF

The date and place of the publication of the first edition are shown in each case. The Hogarth Press are the publishers of Virginia Woolf's work in Britain, and Harcourt, Brace and Company in the United States.

1. Novels

The Voyage Out, London, 1915.
Night and Day, London, 1919.
Jacob's Room, London, 1922.
Mrs. Dalloway, London, 1925.
To the Lighthouse, London, 1927.
Orlando. A Biography, London, 1928.
The Waves, London, 1931.
The Years, London, 1937.
Between the Acts, London, 1941.

2. Short Stories and Sketches

Two Stories (in collaboration with Leonard Woolf), London, 1917.
Kew Gardens, London, 1919.
The Mark on the Wall, London, 1919.
Monday or Tuesday, London, 1921.

3. Essays and Critical Writings

Mr. Bennett and Mrs. Brown, London, 1924.

The Common Reader, London, 1925.

Victorian Photographs of Famous Men and Fair Women, by J. M. Cameron. With introductions by Roger Fry and Virginia Woolf, London, 1926.

A Sentimental Journey through France and Italy, by Lawrence Sterne. With an introduction by Virginia Woolf, Oxford University Press (World's Classics Series), 1928.

A Room of One's Own, London, 1929.

On Being Ill, London, 1930. (First printed in the *New Criterion,* January, 1926.)

Beau Brummell, New York, 1930.

Street Haunting, London, 1930.

Life As We Have Known It, by Cooperative Women. Edited by M. L. Davies. With an introduction by Virginia Woolf. London, 1931.

The Common Reader. Second Series, London, 1932. (American title: *The Second Common Reader.*)

A Letter to a Young Poet, London, 1932.

Walter Sickert, a Conversation, London, 1934.

Three Guineas, London, 1938.

The Death of the Moth, New York, 1942.

The Moment and Other Essays, London, 1947.

The Captain's Death-Bed, London, 1950.

Granite and Rainbow, London, 1958.

4. Biographies

Flush. A Biography, London, 1933.

Roger Fry. A Biography, London, 1940.

5. Diary and Letters

A Writer's Diary, Being Extracts from the Diary of Virginia Woolf, London, 1953.

Virginia Woolf and Lytton Strachey—Letters, London, 1956.

BIBLIOGRAPHY

6. Translations

Dostoevsky, *Stavrogin's Confession*. Translated into English by S. S. Koteliansky and Virginia Woolf, London, 1922.

Goldenveizer, A. B. *Talks with Tolstoi*. Translated by S. S. Koteliansky and Virginia Woolf, London, 1923.

Tolstoi's Love Letters. With a study of the autobiographical elements in Tolstoi's work, by Paul Birkuyov. Translated by S. S. Koteliansky and Virginia Woolf, London, 1923.

II. CRITICAL STUDIES

Bennett, Joan, *Virginia Woolf: Her Art as a Novelist*, 1945.

Blackstone, Bernard, *Virginia Woolf: A Commentary*, 1948.

Chambers, R. L., *The Novels of Virginia Woolf*, 1947.

Daiches, David, *The Novel and the Modern World*, 2nd edition, 1960.

Delattre, Floris, *Le Roman Psychologique de Virginia Woolf*, 1932.

Forster, E. M., *Virginia Woolf*, 1942.

Holtby, Winifred, *Virginia Woolf*, 1932.

Johnstone, J. K., *The Bloomsbury Group*, 1954.

Kumar, Shiv, *Bergson and the Stream of Consciousness Novel*, 1962.

III. BIBLIOGRAPHY

Kirkpatrick, B. J., *A Bibliography of Virginia Woolf*, 1957.

Modern Fiction Studies, vol. II, No. 1 (February 1956), Virginia Woolf Special Number, includes checklist of criticism.

INDEX

INDEX

167

INDEX

NEW DIRECTIONS PAPERBOOKS

Corrado Alvaro, *Revolt in Aspromonte* [P 119].
Chairil Anwar, *Selected Poems* [World Poets Series 2].
Djuna Barnes, *Nightwood* [P 98].
Charles Baudelaire, *Flowers of Evil* [P 71].
Eric Bentley, *Bernard Shaw* [P 59].
Alain Bosquet, *Selected Poems* [World Poets Series 4].
Kay Boyle, *Thirty Stories* [P 62].
Breakthrough to Peace, Anthology. Intro. by Th. Merton [P 124].
L.-F. Céline, *Journey to the End of the Night* [P 84].
Bankim-chandra Chatterjee, *Krishnakanta's Will* [P 120].
Maurice Collis, *The Land of the Great Image* [P 76]. *Marco Polo* [P 93].
Gregory Corso, *The Happy Birthday of Death* [P. 86]. *Long Live Man* [P 127].
David Daiches, *Virginia Woolf* [P 137].
William Empson, *Some Versions of Pastoral* [P 92].
Lawrence Ferlinghetti, *A Coney Island of the Mind* [P 74]. *Her* [P 88]. *Starting from San Francisco,* with lp record [Gift Edition, Out of Series].
Ronald Firbank, *Two Novels. The Flower Beneath the Foot & Prancing Nigger* [P 128].
Dudley Fitts, *Poems from the Greek Anthology* [P 60].
F. Scott Fitzgerald, *The Crack-Up* [P 54].
Gustave Flaubert, *Sentimental Education* [P 63].
Andre Gide, *Dostoevsky* [P 100].
Goethe, *Faust, Part I* (MacIntyre translation) [P 70].
Henry Hatfield, *Goethe* [P 136]. *Thomas Mann* [P 101].
John Hawkes, *The Cannibal* [P 123]. *The Lime Twig* [P 95].
Hermann Hesse, *Siddhartha* [P 65].
Edwin Honig, *García Lorca,* rev. ed. [P 102].
Ann Hutchinson, *Labanotation* [P 104].
Christopher Isherwood, *The Berlin Stories* [P 134].
Henry James, *Stories of Artists and Writers* [P 57].
Alfred Jarry, *Ubu Roi* [P 105].
James Joyce, *Stephen Hero* [P 133].
Franz Kafka, *Amerika* [P 117].
Choderlos de Laclos, *Dangerous Acquaintances* [P 61].
Denise Levertov, *The Jacob's Ladder* [P 112].
Harry Levin, *James Joyce: A Critical Introduction* [P 87].
García Lorca, *Selected Poems* [P 114]. *Three Tragedies* [P 52].

Thomas Merton, *Bread in the Wilderness* [P 91]. *Clement of Alexandria* [Gift Edition, Out of Series]. *Selected Poems* [P 85].

Henry Miller, *The Colossus of Maroussi* [P 75]. *The Cosmological Eye* [P 109]. *Remember to Remember* [P 111]. *Sunday After the War* [P 110]. *The Time of the Assassins* [P 115]. *The Wisdom of the Heart* [P 94].

Vladimir Nabokov, *Nikolai Gogol* [P 78].

New Directions, Anthology. No. 11 [P 72]. No. 16 [P 64]. No. 17 [P 103]. *A New Directions Reader* [P 135].

George Oppen, *The Materials* [P 122].

Boris Pasternak, *Safe Conduct* [P 77].

Kenneth Patchen, *Because It Is* [P 83]. *But Even So* [P 132]. *The Journal of Albion Moonlight* [P 99].

Octavio Paz, *Sun Stone* [World Poets Series 1].

Ezra Pound, *ABC of Reading* [P 89]. With Ernest Fenollosa, *The Classic Noh Theatre of Japan* [P 79]. *The Confucian Odes* [P 81]. With Noel Stock, *Love Poems of Ancient Egypt* [Gift Edition, Out of Series]. *Selected Poems* [P 66]. *The Translations* [P 145].

Philip Rahv, *Image and Idea* [P 67].

Kenneth Rexroth, *Assays* [P 113]. *Bird in the Bush* [P 80]. *The Homestead Called Damascus* [World Poets Series 3].

Charles Reznikoff, *By the Waters of Manhattan* [P 121].

Arthur Rimbaud, *Illuminations* [P 56]. *A Season in Hell & The Drunken Boat* [P 97].

Jean-Paul Sartre, *Nausea* [P 82].

Stendhal, *Lucien Leuwen. Book I: The Green Huntsman* [P 107]. *Book II: The Telegraph* [P 108].

Dylan Thomas, *A Child's Christmas in Wales* [Gift Edition, Out of Series]. *Portrait of the Artist as a Young Dog* [P 51]. *Quite Early One Morning* [P 90]. *Under Milk Wood* [P 73].

Norman Thomas, *Ask at the Unicorn* [P 129].

Nathanael West, *Miss Lonelyhearts & The Day of the Locust* [P 125].

William Carlos Williams, *In the American Grain* [P 53]. *The Farmers' Daughters* [P 106]. *Pictures from Brueghel and Other Poems* [P 118]. *Selected Poems* [P 131].

Send for free catalog describing all Paperbooks

NEW DIRECTIONS   333 Sixth Avenue   New York 14